Meeting the
National Standards
with Handbells
and Handchimes

Michael B. McBride
and Marva Baldwin

The Scarecrow Press, Inc.
Lanham, Maryland, and London
2000

SCARECROW PRESS, INC.

Published in the United States of America
by Scarecrow Press, Inc.
4720 Boston Way, Lanham, Maryland 20706
http://www.scarecrowpress.com

4 Pleydell Gardens, Folkestone
Kent CT20 2DN, England

British Library Cataloguing in Publication Information Available

Library of Congress Cataloging-in-Publication Data

McBride, Michael B.
 Meeting the national standards with handbells and handchimes / Michael
B. McBride and Marva Baldwin.
  p. cm.
 Includes bibliographic references.
 ISBN 0-8108-3740-4 (p : alk. paper)
  1. Handbell ringing—Standards. 2. Handbells—Instruction and study.
3. Handchimes—Instruction and study. I. Baldwin, Marva. II. Title.

MT711.M35   2000
786.8′8485193′071073—dc21   99-054130
                                            CIP

Contents

Reprint Permission

The following permissions are granted to any person, organization, or other entity wishing to reprint or duplicate portions of the National Standards for Arts Education:

> Permission to reprint all or part of the summary statement (pages 131-133).
> Permission to reprint all or part of the content standards.
> Permission to reprint quotations of up to fifty words from the introductory materials (pages 5-19).

All copies of material duplicated from the Standards must include the following credit line:

> From National Standards for Arts Education.

Biographical Sketches

Michael B. McBride has been a music educator for over twenty-five years serving both in the classroom (K-12) and as music coordinator in central administration. Currently serving as an adjunct faculty member at the University of Colorado at Boulder, Dr. McBride is a frequent conductor, clinician, recitalist, and adjudicator throughout the nation. At the present time he has four handbell compositions in print and is a frequent contributor to music education publications. After completing his bachelor's degree in music performance at the University of Denver and completing his master's in music performance at the University of Colorado at Boulder, Dr. McBride completed his Ph.D. in music education at the University of Denver. He has been a church musician (organist/choir director/handbell director) for over thirty years, during which time he has directed handbell choirs that toured nationally, appeared on television specials, and released commercial tapes. He is a member of The National Association for Music Education (MENC); Colorado Music Educators Association (CMEA), where he served for eight years as executive secretary/treasurer; American Choral Directors Association (ACDA); American Guild of Organists (AGO); and the American Guild of English Handbell Ringers (AGEHR), where he has served on various committees in Area XI, as well as a clinician for Colorado. At the present time he serves on the Education Committee of the Colorado Symphony Orchestra.

Marva Baldwin is a music education specialist presently teaching general music at Marshdale Elementary School in Evergreen, Colorado. Ms. Baldwin has taught music in Iowa, Wisconsin, Ohio, and in the Jefferson County School District in Colorado for the past twenty-five years. With an undergraduate degree in music education from Luther College, Decorah, Iowa, she earned her master's of arts degree from the University of Colorado at Denver. She has been recognized by her school as "Teacher of the Year." She presently teaches eighteen classes of music and art, directs the fifth grade "Honor Ringers," and co-sponsors the Council for the Arts and Humanities. Ms. Baldwin is a member of The National Association for Music Education (MENC) and National, Colorado and Jefferson County Education Associations. Ms. Baldwin has been the AGEHR Area XI Colorado Chimes and Handbells in Music Education (CHIME) chairman, as well as a frequent clinician at handbell conferences. She has played handbells with the University of Colorado Alumni Handbell Ensemble. In addition to directing the Marshdale School handbell choir, she also directs the "Mountain Ringers," an auditioned community handbell ensemble, and the Evergreen Lutheran Church Chime Choir. She is chairman of the Mountain Community Handbell Coalition and recently served on the Jefferson County School District's Writing Team for Music Content Standards.

Kermit Junkert is national director of handbells for Schulmerich Bells, where his responsibilities include the coordination and development of resources that foster the use of handbells throughout the world. He also contributes toward the further development of handbell innovations and accessories. Under his leadership, a five-person task force produced "Handbells in the Liturgy," a comprehensive resource book published by Concordia Publishing House. He has taught at numerous AGEHR National Director's Seminars; the 7th International Handbell Symposium, Albuquerque, New Mexico, and the 8th International Symposium in Makuhari, Japan. As a master handbell technician, he is one of the leading experts in repair and refurbishment of handbells and is frequently called upon as a teacher. He is the creator of the popular "Bell Mastery Series," a series of classes that are taught from the perspective of the handbell, bringing a better understanding of the instrument, thus producing more artistic playing. He has a degree in music education from the University of Minnesota and has been involved in church music and education programs since 1970. He is a member of AGEHR.

Phyllis Treby Hentz, music director for Schulmerich Bells, arranges and records music for Schulmerich carillon products, acts as music consultant for all departments, conducts handbell workshops, and directs the employee handbell choir. She directs an age and ability graded handbell program of five choirs. Her advanced adult choir, the Jubilation Ringers, has aired on PBS television and National Public Radio. She is a frequent clinician and guest conductor with several handbell compositions in print.

Donna Kinsey is pastoral musician for the parish of St. Theresa and music teacher (K-9) for St. Francis Central School, Morgantown, West Virginia. She has served as state chair and as a board member in Area V of the AGEHR, and has served on the National Board of the Catholic Music Educators. She received her bachelor's of science from Indiana University of Pennsylvania and her master's of music education from West Virginia University.

Karen Pfiffner is director of the handbell program at the University of Colorado at Boulder. With over twenty years of ringing/directing experience, she directs multiple handbell ensembles and is a frequent lecturer and clinician. She has served as a board member for the Colorado Chapter of AGEHR. She is a graduate of the University of Colorado at Boulder.

Acknowledgments

Recognizing that no one can claim to be truly educated who lacks basic knowledge and skills in the arts, Schulmerich Bells supports a comprehensive, sequential music education program that is taught by qualified individuals. Students actively involved in a music education program develop self-discipline and artistic problem solving. They experience a sense of accomplishment and achievement with a completed product and develop the skills necessary for life-long participation in a musical activity.

Regardless of physical or artistic abilities, all students have the opportunity to be an active participant in music education programs providing value and significance for daily living. Assessment of individuals and performing ensembles is an integral part of every music program.

Schulmerich Bells believes that the use of handbells and hand-held chimes (handchimes) is a vital contributor toward the fulfillment of the National Standards. Whether used in a supportive role in a general music class or as a highly developed musical ensemble, handbells provide a full measure of musical enjoyment for all who play them, and for all who listen.

In the preparation of this book, Schulmerich would like to thank the following: Concordia, for the release of material found in *Handbells & the Liturgy*, Donna Kinsey, for her contributions to the early development of this book; Karen Pfiffner, for her contributions of literature and ideas for advanced ringers; and Phyllis Hentz, music director for Schulmerich Bells, for her review of manuscripts and contributions. Particular appreciation is given to Michael McBride for conceptualizing this book and Marva Baldwin for writing and bringing the concept to finality. Kermit Junkert, national director of handbells for Schulmerich Bells, deserves special recognition for his review and coordination with the authors.

Schulmerich Bells is committed to the continued development of excellence in music education programs throughout the world, and we see this book as one of many contributions that we have made. We trust that the use of this book, along with your handbells and handchimes, will fulfill your goal of meeting the National Standards for Music Education.

Bern E. Deichmann, President & CEO
Schulmerich Bells

MENC–The National Association for Music Education believes that every young American, pre-kindergarten through grade 12, should receive a balanced, comprehensive, sequential, and high-quality music education taught by qualified teachers. As illustrated in this volume, a handbell and handchime program can be an effective means for music educators to help students work toward meeting the National Standards for Music Education – the foundation for a strong music curriculum. Using the increasingly varied repertoire available to players of handbells and handchimes, music educators will find *Meeting the National Standards with Handbells and Handchimes* to be a practical guide for building programs that meet the needs of individual students in our nation's schools.

John J. Mahlmann, Executive Director
MENC–The National Association for
Music Education

Introduction

Schulmerich – Meeting the National Standards with Handbells and Handchimes

National Content Standards for Music Education

1. Singing, alone and with others, a varied repertoire of music
2. Performing on instruments, alone and with others, a varied repertoire of music
3. Improvising melodies, variations, and accompaniments
4. Composing and arranging music within specified guidelines
5. Reading and notating music
6. Listening to, analyzing, and describing music
7. Evaluating music and music performances
8. Understanding relationships between music, the other arts, and disciplines outside the arts
9. Understanding music in relation to history and culture

The National Standards in Arts Education (dance, music, theater, visual arts) help children, parents, educators, and the community realize the value and importance of music in our society today. Students that participate in a standards-based music education program benefit since music helps to "cultivate the whole child, gradually building many kinds of literacy while developing intuition, reasoning, imagination, and dexterity into unique forms of expression and communication. The process requires not merely an active mind but a trained one." (National Standards for Arts Education, p. 6)

As a part of the Standards' process, each state, and in some states, each school district, is to establish standards for the state or district level. State and local standards are to meet or exceed the National Standards. Many states have modified the number of standards, generally reducing the number. In reviewing the states' Arts Standards, it is noted that they contain the elements found in the National Arts Standards. For this publication, the nine National

Music Standards have been combined into five music content standards using handbells and/or handchimes. The five standards developed for this publication state that students will possess the ability to (1) perform, alone and in ensembles, a varied repertoire of handbell/handchime music; (2) read and notate handbell music; (3) listen, respond, evaluate, and describe handbell music; (4) create music with handbells and/or handchimes; and (5) use handbells and/or handchimes to understand the relationship music has with other disciplines as well as in history and culture. Educators are encouraged to parallel the appropriate chapter (standard) to their own district, state, or the National Standard.

Many music educators have taught to standards for years – their own standards or standards developed by a faculty or school district. The National Standards support accountability toward an advanced level of achievement for educators and students.

Handbell and/or handchime programs exist in many settings (educational, religious, and community) and vary in ability level from rote ringers to very sophisticated, musically knowledgeable ringers. In the field of education, the successes and goal-reaching possibilities when handbells and/or handchimes are included in the school music program are becoming more widely recognized. The use of these instruments supports positive learning experiences for young children and special learners to advanced university ringers and master ringers. Handbells and/or handchimes are exceptionally fine tools for not only learning musical concepts but also for learning physical, mental, and social skills. Even though both are generally thought of as ensemble instruments, handchimes in particular can encompass a wider usage among young children, special learners, and the elderly. Listening skills and attention span noticeably improve. The development and refinement of coordination improves as does singing and pitch accuracy. As an individual ringer or in an ensemble setting, life-long learning skills, such as flexibility, critical thinking, and problem solving, are developed. Ringers learn to apply the skills of collaboration, communication, and cooperation.

This publication assumes that educators are knowledgeable about basic ringing techniques for handchimes and/or handbells. The format of this book includes a rationale which explains the purpose and general structure of the publication. Each standard, a description of what each student is expected to know, is then presented in a chapter with an introduction and key points (components). In Chapters 1-3, the key points are developed by a series of benchmarks – descriptions of the knowledge or skills expected at various developmental levels (Levels I–VI) in order for a student to demonstrate mastery of the standard.

Levels I–VI are presented with the understanding that achievement is dependent on experience, maturation, and desire to improve, as well as the quality of instruction received. Generally speaking, Level I corresponds to Beginner, Level II to Advanced Beginner, Level III to Intermediate, Level IV to Proficient, Level V to Advanced, and Level VI to the Master ringer status. These levels are not to be confused with the AGEHR publication, "Handbell Notation Difficulty Level System," which is designed to determine the difficulty of handbell and/or handchime music. Directors must start where the ringers are and make musical and handbell and/or handchime technique adjustments as needed. If directors and students utilize these lessons as a basis for understanding the elements of the standards, individual ringers in the handbell and/or handchime ensemble will not only meet the National Standards, but the director will be able to assess progress on a student-by-student basis. The Examples for Meaning, including strategies and samples of music repertoire, are aligned to assist the director or teacher and student in achieving the concept of each benchmark.

It is hoped that this publication will be a helpful resource to the director/educator in his or her quest for excellence in teaching today's students with handbells and/or handchimes. It is further hoped that handbells and/or handchimes will become an integral part of the complete music education program in every educational setting.

Chapter 1

Introduction to Handbells and Handchimes

Music education programs are a core part of the school curriculum and provide numerous benefits. The use of handbells and handchimes supports the nine National Standards for Music Education, which in turn support many causes, such as musicianship, teamwork, and self-expression. Music educators find handbells and handchimes to be an effective means for educating children, as well as a public relations tool.

Development of a Plan

The initial step in establishing a handbell and/or handchime program is the development of a strategy. This plan would include establishing the purpose of such a program, short- and long-range goals and objectives, as well as the funding and ultimate purchase of the equipment. Other requirements would be the placement in the curriculum, faculty staffing, and recruitment of ringers. If your administration and parents are not familiar with handbells and handchimes, invite a local handbell choir to present a concert. You may want to attend a handbell concert in your area or volunteer as a substitute at a handbell rehearsal. Also, you could invite a handbell manufacturer's representative to come and talk to your interest group.

There are many available resources, one of which is the American Guild of English Handbell Ringers (AGEHR). This is a national organization dedicated to providing director/teacher and ringer training and education for its members. AGEHR has formed a standing committee for education – Chimes and Handbells in Music Education (CHIME), which in turn develops programs to support teachers, publishes an education newsletter, and coordinates an outstanding ringer recognition program. For further information, including membership forms, contact the AGEHR National Office (1-800-878-5459) in Dayton, Ohio.

Fund-Raising and the Purchase of Equipment

While handbells and handchimes can be relatively expensive, they are a good investment. For the cost of some orchestral instruments used by only one person, an entire three-octave set of handbells (C4-C7) can be purchased and creatively used by eleven to twenty-two ringers at the same time. Handchimes, which are less expensive, may be used as an alternative instrument.

If financial support is not possible through the school system, other sources of funding should be considered. Creating a partnership with a local business can be very worthwhile. Fund-raising can take the shape of cake walks, T-shirt sales, or performances for donations – the list of ideas is limited only by your imagination. Individual or group gifts are frequently made for individual bells and/or octaves of handbells and handchimes. The pursuit and recognition of patrons or sponsors could be a job for a parent or parents of a choir member.

Handbells and Handchimes, Equipment and Accessories
(Tables/Covers, Foam, Binders/Risers, Gloves, Mallets)

While handbells have been designed and constructed to be suitable for classroom applications, handbells can be damaged with reckless treatment. As with any quality instrument, utmost care and respect should be given. Since handbells are a bronze alloy and are polished to a jeweler's finish, it is recommended that ringers wear gloves to protect the handbell finish. After each use, handbells should be freed from fingerprints and moisture by using a polishing cloth. Proper playing techniques will prevent bells from clanging together, which might cause bell casting damage.

There is one primary decision to be made when purchasing handbells. Some handbell manufacturers offer a choice of two clapper assemblies: Quick-Adjust™ or Select-A-Strike™ clapper assemblies. Clapper heads are designed with several timbre settings to achieve optimum blend between handbells. By the rotation of the clapper head, these settings can be selected. Each style of clapper assembly has distinct advantages and should be investigated and researched before purchasing your set of handbells.

Guardian discs or handguard discs are placed between the handbell casting and the handle for the purpose of keeping the ringer's hand from touching the casting and damping the sound. MasterTouch™ Discs have been ergonomically designed to conform better to the shape of the ringer's hand, thus reducing hand fatigue and relieving stress points. Historically, handguard discs and handles were black, but recently manufacturers have begun to provide "black and gold" colors to identify diatonic notes from accidental notes, thus facilitating the ringer's visualization of their respective handbell assignments. Also, consult the manufacturer's care and maintenance manual concerning additional care ideas and to assist you with the setting of tension and other related items.

Like handbells, handchimes should be treated with the utmost care and respect. Adjustments can be made to optimize precision response and tonal qualities. Handchimes have a number of advantages over handbells in that ringers do not need to wear gloves, nor do the handchimes need to be polished. Handchimes are ideal as a beginning instrument, or they may be used as an alternative voice within a handbell choir.

Tables come in a variety of shapes and sizes. When selecting tables, recognize that they must be sturdy, yet portable. While ordinary banquet tables may be used, they are difficult to handle and are too low for adults to ring off of comfortably. Ideally, handbell tables for adults should be 36" long by 30" wide by 32" high. Tables with adjustable legs are very useful for two reasons: (1) they may be adjusted for use by a children's handbell choir or for an adult handbell choir, and (2) adjustments may be made for unusual ringing situations where a step may be in the way or the floor is uneven.

Suggested minimum linear feet of table space:

Two octaves	15 linear feet
Three octaves	21 linear feet
Four octaves	24 linear feet
Five octaves	30 linear feet
Six octaves	39 linear feet

Four inches of supersoft foam is recommended for use with today's handbell ringing techniques. While directors have varying opinions about the density of foam, be aware that it is easier to damp handbells in soft foam (particularly the lower octaves), but if the foam is too soft, certain stopped sound techniques may cause damage to the handbells.

Table covers are available commercially or can be custom made. They are needed not only for aesthetic reasons but also to prevent the tarnish that can result from direct placement on foam. Pinwale corduroy is a popular and preferred fabric and should be used with the pattern running vertically rather than horizontally. While any material can be used, select a material that is neither too slippery nor too rough and one that does not inhibit the sound. This is frequently the case with synthetic fabric.

Handbell and/or handchime choirs use special three-ring flex music binder stands that sit on top of the table to hold the music. Music is three-hole punched and inserted in the notebook. Normally one stand is used for every two ringers. Many choirs raise the music for easier reading by using music risers. Risers are constructed from a variety of material including textured black steel, clear acrylic, or wood.

Ringers should wear gloves at all times to prevent tarnish and etching of the handbell finish by hand and finger marks. Gloves also protect the ringer's hands and provide a comfortable cushion while holding the handbell. Gloves come in a variety of styles and colors, ranging from plain cotton to plastic dot performance gloves. Since they are washable, gloves should be bought one size larger to allow for shrinkage.

Mallets are available in a variety of octave configurations to reproduce the distinctive tonal quality of each bell. Mallets, which have not been designed for handbells or for a particular handbell, might cause damage to that bell casting.

	Two Octaves	Three Octaves	Four Octaves	Five Octaves	Six Octaves
G2-F#3	-	-	-	2	3
G3-E4	-	2	3	3	3
F4-B4	2	2	2	2	2
C5-A#5	3	3	3	3	3
B5-F#6	2	2	2	2	2
G6-G7	1	2	3	3	3
G#7-G8	-	-	-	2	4

Figure 1.1

Personnel Selection

Individuals who wish to become a handbell and/or handchime director need to be enthusiastic and committed to developing and administering a comprehensive program. They will take the time to learn the necessary techniques to direct a handbell and/or handchime choir successfully. Ideally, the handbell and/or handchime director in the school setting should be a licensed certificated music educator. The handbell director must, at the very least, be musical and have basic music skills. Fundamental conducting skills are necessary and keyboard skills are helpful. Knowledge of handbell ringing skills and symbols unique to handbell literature are essential. AGEHR sponsors excellent workshops and seminars for directors and ringers.

While anyone can play handbells, not everyone will achieve the same degree of success. The director must predetermine objectives, such as the main purpose and what is to be accomplished, and personnel must be selected to meet those objectives. A long-range plan should be implemented to include beginning, intermediate, and advanced ringers with instruction at each level as a preparation for advancement. Handchimes are very appropriate at the primary level, with handbells introduced at the intermediate level. In addition to classroom use of handbells and handchimes, smaller numbers of ten to twelve dedicated ringers could be organized to form a handbell and/or handchime choir. Ringers may be selected in a variety of ways, such as grade level or musical ability level. It is advisable to screen potential ringers on an individual basis to learn their past experience and potential. An effective handbell choir program may challenge even the best musicians, whether they are in kindergarten, middle school, high school, or are adults.

Handbell and/or Handchime Assignments

A set of handbells and/or handchimes is chromatic and, for the beginner, should be placed in keyboard order, that is, diatonically from the ringers' left to right. Handbell and handchime assignments should be based on an individual's musical ability and the director's desire to keep them as busy as is practical and realistic, i.e., ringing often. For early beginners, it is suggested that each student hold one handbell or handchime. As players develop even minimal skills, the most common assignment is to give each player two adjacent notes (C and D), with that person having responsibility for the related accidentals. Notes may also be assigned at the octave (D6 and D7), with accidentals assigned as needed. With a number of other assignment methods in use with both beginner and advanced ensembles, the director is encouraged to explore alternative assignments based on student ability and the musical effect desired.

Handbell Basics

In a first rehearsal with a group of would-be-ringers, show them how to hold a bell and how to ring and damp correctly. Giving verbal instructions instead of depending on the written page, ring a few short exercises. These exercises or drills should consist of ringing simple chords,

striving to ring the chord tones together, learning to ring repeated notes and chords, and learning to damp the bells correctly. Ringers may also play single-line scale passages, emphasizing learning to ring individually at the proper time, learning to damp at the proper time, and learning to make the sound of one's handbell or handchime match that of the neighbor. After doing these basic drills, gradually introduce ringers to the written page.

In ringing a handbell, grasp the handle firmly with your hand against the handguard, wrapping your fingers around the handle. Hold the bell upright, tipping it slightly toward your shoulder so the clapper falls toward the shoulder. The range of ringing should be above the waist, but below the shoulder. Move the bell down flexing the wrist as the bell reaches the forward part of the motion while keeping the bell slightly forward of vertical. After the clapper strikes the bell, return the bell to the shoulder by continuing a circular motion. To damp the bell, press it gently against your shoulder. As soon as it is damped, move it back to a ringing position. The more rapid the ringing, the closer the bell will stay to the shoulder.

Figure 1.2

Handchime Basics

In order to balance the handchime in your hand, grasp it slightly below the identifying pitch plate and cock the open end of the chime back toward your chest so that the clapper falls back toward your shoulder. With the closed end of the handchime pointed downward and away from you, lead the chime away from your body with the closed end. The motion of the handchime should emulate that of a handbell with the strike point at the vertical position. The clapper will strike the handchime and immediately fall away. Once the chime is struck, you should proceed by lifting the chime back toward your body in an oval backward wheel formation. To damp the handchime, bring it to your chest, turning your arm inward so that both tines touch the chest. Handchimes may also be damped by placing them directly on the table foam, being careful not to restrike the handchime. As with handbells, the larger the instrument, the greater the damping surface required.

Figure 1.3

Chapter 2

Using Handbells and/or Handchimes to Play a Varied Repertoire of Music

Using handbells and/or handchimes to play a varied repertoire of music provides the student with the means of developing musical knowledge and skills. Learning to make music with handbells and/or handchimes enables students to attain individual/ensemble goals, to develop artistic sensitivity, and to acquire basic life-long learning skills.

The development of skills is a cumulative process of the physical experience of ringing and damping handbells and/or handchimes. Growth in playing occurs with regular and continuous opportunities to apply skills to increasingly challenging handbell and/or handchime music literature.

Key Components

In order to meet this standard, handbell and/or handchime students will:
- play using musical elements employing rhythm, melody, harmony, tempo, form, and expressive elements;
- demonstrate appropriate use of playing skills in order to achieve accurate sound production;
- play music of varied cultures, genres, and styles; and
- demonstrate appropriate ensemble skills when performing with others.

The concepts of the key components will be further developed within the following benchmarks.

Benchmarks

Level I – Beginner

Level II – Advanced Beginner

Level III – Intermediate

As students demonstrate beginning handbell and/or handchime playing skills they will:

A. play and distinguish between songs with no beat and songs with a steady beat while gradually developing the ability to make bell, technique, rhythm, and meter changes;

Examples for Meaning:

Level I (Beginner): Randomly ring pitches of a pentatonic scale while singing or listening (see Figures 2.1-2.2).

Level II (Advanced Beginner): Play a steady beat and tempo while listening or while others sing (see Figure 2.3). See also "Amazing Grace" by John Behnke in Appendix G.

Teddy Bear

PENTATONIC   Traditional

TED-DY BEAR TED-DY BEAR,   TURN A - ROUND   TED- DY BEAR,   TED- DY BEAR

Figure 2.1

2.1 **Teddy Bear**, cont.

TOUCH THE   GROUND   TED-DY BEAR,   TED-DY BEAR,   SHOW YOUR   SHOE,

TED-DY BEAR,   TED-DY BEAR,   THAT   WILL   DO.

All Night, All Day

Bells used for improvisation   Bells used for melody

pp

Spiritual

All   night,   all   day,   An -   gels

watch-ing o-ver   me, my   Lord,   All   night,   all

day,   An -   gels   watch-ing o-ver   me.

Figure 2.2

Sarasponda

Dutch Spinning Song
arr. D. Linda McKechnie

Figure 2.3

Level III (Intermediate): Maintain a steady beat while musically playing the strong and weak beats of a song and making basic bell and technique changes (see Figure 2.4). See also "Etude in G" and "Etude in C" by John Behnke in Appendix G.

Sarasponda

Dutch Spinning Song
arr. D. Linda McKechnie

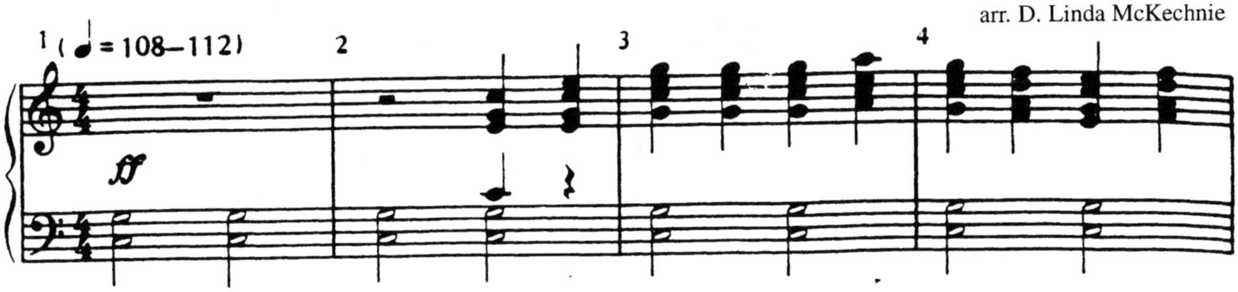

Figure 2.4

Level IV (Proficient): Demonstrate the ability to maintain a steady beat, change tempo, and make more complex bell and technique changes (see Figure 2.5).

Level V (Advanced): Show the ability to maintain the steady pulse while playing various rhythms, tempos, and making rapid handbell and/or handchime and technique changes (see Figure 2.6).

Kum Ba Ya

Spiritual
arr. John F. Wilson

Figure 2.5

The Entertainer

Scott Joplin
arr. Sharon Elery Rogers

Figure 2.6

Level VI (Master): Demonstrate mastery at making numerous handbell and technique changes while playing correct rhythms and tempos (see Figure 2.7).

Antiphonal Alleluia

Hart Morris

Figure 2.7

B. demonstrate proper execution of technique skills to achieve accurate sound production and expressive qualities;

Examples for Meaning:

Level I: While demonstrating correct posture and good playing position, strike the handbell or handchime precisely on the beat and follow through with an "oval" motion, damping for precise termination of the sound (see Figure 2.8).

Level II: Strike and damp the handbell or handchime with correct technique while observing duration, phrasing, and dynamics of notes and rests in the melody and/or harmony (see Figure 2.9). See also "A Scottish Melody" by John Behnke in Appendix G.

Figure 2.8

Figure 2.9

Level III: Musically play with expression and technical accuracy (see Figure 2.10). See also "Etude in G minor" by John Behnke in Appendix G.

Level IV: Musically play complex rhythms and techniques while refining expressive elements (see Figure 2.11).

Surprise Symphony

Franz Joseph Haydn
arr. Kevin McChesney

Figure 2.10

Rhapsody on a Theme of Paganini

Serge Rachmaninoff
transcribed by Hart Morris

Figure 2.11

Level V: Demonstrate the ability to use advanced technical skills and to make more rapid changes in musical expression, changing meters and tempo subtleties (see Figure 2.12).

Level VI: Demonstrate virtuosity in musicianship and in the use of technical skills to achieve artistic performance (see Figure 2.13). See also "America the Beautiful" and "Swing Low, Sweet Chariot" by John Behnke in Appendix G.

Fiesta

Barbara Baltzer Kinyon

Figure 2.12

Allegro Festivo

Karen Buckwalter

Figure 2.13

C. demonstrate ensemble skills by playing with others, various forms of music and/or other instruments;

Examples for Meaning:

Level I: Play with others, a single chord or an ostinato pattern while matching and blending timbres and singing a round or canon by rote (see Figures 2.14 and 2.15). See also "Dona Nobis Pacem" by John Behnke in Appendix G.

Level II: Play with others, notes of basic chords to a familiar tune or theme. Apply music reading skills to play variations (see Figure 2.16).

Star Light, Star Bright

Traditional

Figure 2.14

Alleluia (Canon)

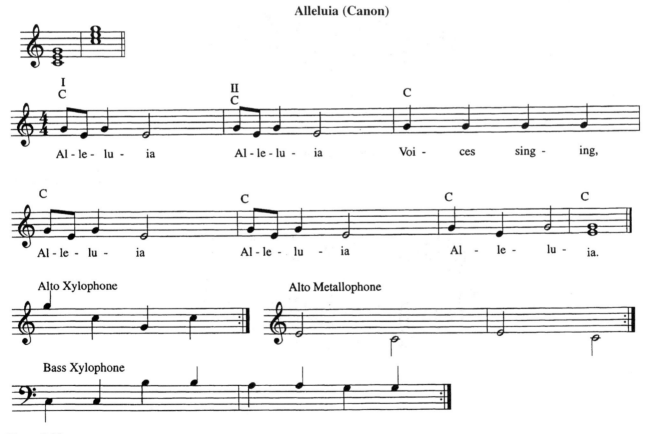

Figure 2.15

Jacob's Ladder I

American Folk Hymn
arr. Martha Lynn Thompson

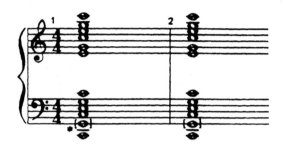

Jacob's Ladder II

American Folk Hymn
arr. Martha Lynn Thompson

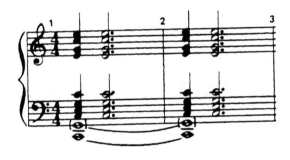

Jacob's Ladder III

American Folk Hymn
arr. Martha Lynn Thompson

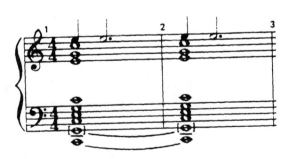

Figure 2.16

Level III: Play with others, in rhythmic unity and balance, with a keyboard instrument or with a vocal choir. Share in the responsibilities of handbell and/or handchime equipment maintenance and functions of the group (see Figures 2.17 and 2.18).

Level IV: Demonstrate musicality and artistic sensitivity while playing with another handbell and/or handchime choir or keyboard instrument. Take an active role in the ensemble's operation (see Figure 2.19).

Level V: Musically respond to the conductor's cues and to a soloist while playing with ensemble members. Take a leadership role in conducting the group's business and performance protocol (see Figure 2.20).

Level VI: Demonstrate well developed ensemble skills and responsiveness to the music and to the conductor while participating in a mass ringing festival, performance or concert setting (see Figure 2.21).

Sheep May Safely Graze

J. S. Bach
arr. Barbara Kinyon

Figure 2.17

Seasonal Procession (for Christmas or Easter)

Cynthia Dobrinski

Figure 2.18

Echo Rondo

Everett Jay Hilty

Figure 2.19

Bandelier

Tammy W. Rawlinson
(ASCAP)

Figure 2.20

Fanfare & Procession

Kevin L. Shull

Figure 2.21

D. play an expanding repertoire of music representing various cultures, genres, and styles.

Examples for Meaning:

Level I: Ring a variety of handbell or handchime repertoire while others sing, play ethnic instruments, and/or move appropriately to the action words (see Figures 2.22 and 2.23).

Level II: Play a moving bass and/or chords and appropriately interpret diverse styles of music (see Figures 2.24 and 2.25).

Level III: Perform music representative of other cultures and countries with expression appropriate for the work being performed (see Figure 2.26).

Level IV: Show artistic sensitivity and technical skill in playing a wide variety of distinctive styles of music (see Figure 2.27). See also "Sometimes I Feel Like a Motherless Child" by John Behnke in Appendix G.

Kuma San

Japanese Folk Song

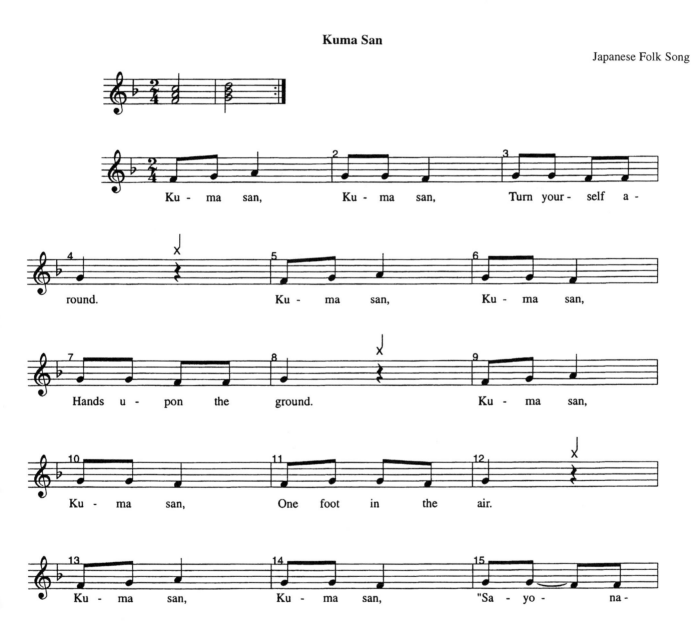

Figure 2.22

Zum Gali Gali

Israeli Work Song

Figure 2.23

The German Folk Song

arr. D. Linda McKechnie

Figure 2.24

The Boogie Woogie Ghost

Nadine M. Peglar

Use mallets throughout.

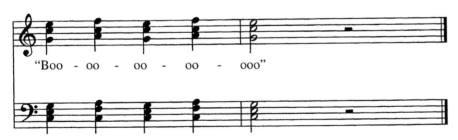

"Boo - oo - oo - oo - ooo"

Figure 2.25

Takeda Rhapsody

Based on an old song of the Kyoto district in Japan

Figure 2.26

Go Down Moses

Traditional Spiritual
arr. Hart Morris

Figure 2.27

Level V: Display musicality and technical competency by ringing complex notational markings that authentically interpret the specific genre of music (see Figure 2.28). See also "Shalom, My Friends" by John Behnke in Appendix G.

Level VI: Perform with expression and technical accuracy a large and varied repertoire that is representative of other cultures and countries (see Figure 2.29). See also "An Irish Melody" by John Behnke in Appendix G.

Can Can

Gioacchino Rossini
transcribed Philip M. Young

Figure 2.28

Hava Nageela

Israeli Folk Song
arr. Douglas Floyd Smith

Figure 2.29

Chapter 3

Reading and Notating Music

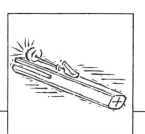

S tudents will read and play music while using handbells and/or handchimes.

Introduction

The knowledge and understanding of music notation is essential to music literacy. A sequential method of learning music notation must be adopted by the director/teacher, and the individual player's progress must be continuously monitored. Unlike a choral ensemble where, with the support of the other members of the section, one "no-reader" can still be effective, handbell and/or handchime ringers are a section unto themselves and must stand on their own. The ringer in an ensemble has his or her own obligations and opportunities. The individual ringer is not only responsible for his or her own notes and dynamics but must also develop a "team mentality" to accurately play and interpret the music with the ensemble.

In meeting National Standard #2, students will be able to read music, ring, and apply the traditional, as well as the distinctive notation devices of handbell ringing techniques. It is understood that student progress is cumulative from level to level.

Key Components

In order to meet this standard, students will:

- read and sight-read traditional music notation;
- identify, define, and apply traditional and handbell music notational symbols and terminology; and
- read and demonstrate proper execution of traditional and handbell and/or handchime music articulation technique symbols.

The concepts of the key components will be further developed within the following benchmarks.

Benchmarks

Level I – Beginner
Level II – Advanced Beginner
Level III – Intermediate
Level IV – Proficient
Level V – Advanced
Level VI – Master

As students demonstrate music skills in reading traditional notation, ringing handbell symbols, and applying notational devices of handbell techniques, they will:

A. identify, read, and ring pitches of the Grand Staff and rhythm patterns using whole, half, quarter, eighth, sixteenth, dotted notes, and rests in simple and complex meters;

Examples for Meaning;

Level I: Demonstrate the ability to ring and damp two bells or chimes together and separately, playing accurate duration and making an "elliptical" motion (lift and float) after ringing the bell (see Figure 3.1).

Level II: Show the ability to use two handbells or handchimes to play a variety of music. Give full value to each note and rest. Damp the bell on the next beat. Do not damp repeated notes. Ring the exercise slowly at first, increasing the tempo gradually (see Figures 3.2a–3.2d).

Level III: Demonstrate the ability to accurately ring and damp two bells or chimes reading a variety of music with simple meters (see Figure 3.3).

Level IV: Demonstrate proficiency in ringing three or more bells in changing rhythms, time, and key (major or minor) signatures (see Figure 3.4).

Level V: Demonstrate advanced skills in playing four or more bells of both clefs in music with quickly changing rhythms, time, and key signatures (see Figure 3.5).

Level VI: Demonstrate mastery in playing five or more bells of both clefs while reading very advanced handbell music (see Figure 3.6).

Twinkle, Twinkle Little Star

Traditional
arr. Martha Lynn Thompson

Figure 3.1

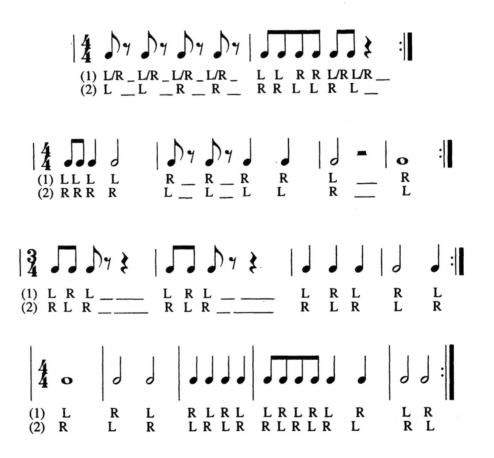

Figure 3.2a

Twinkle, Twinkle, Little Star

Traditional
arr. Martha Lynn Thompson

Figure 3.2b

Crusader's Hymn

arr. Beverly Simpson

Figure 3.2c

**Aloha One
(Farewell to Thee)**

Queen Liliuokalani
arr. Frances L. Callahan

Figure 3.2d

(1) L   R   L   R   L   R   L   R
(2) R   L   R   L   R   L   R   L

(1) R   R   L   _   R   R   L   L L R
(2) L   L   R   _   L   L   R   R R L

(1) L   R L   R   L R   L   L   R L   R
(2) R   L R   L   R L   R   L   R L   L

(1) L   R L R   L   R L   R   _ L R L R L   R   L R
(2) R   L R L   R   L R   L   _ R L R L R   L   R L

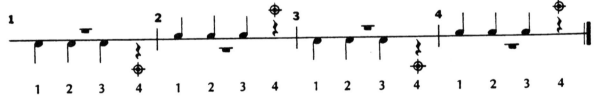

1   2   3   4   1   2   3   4   1   2   3   4   1   2   3   4

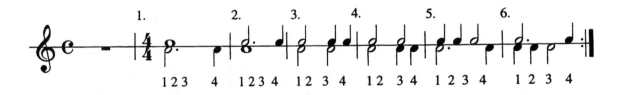

1 2 3   4   1 2 3 4   1 2   3   4   1 2   3   4   1 2 3 4   1 2   3   4

Figure 3.3

Down by the Riverside

Arnold Sherman

Figure 3.4

Send In the Clowns

Stephen Sondheim
arr. Douglas Wagner

Figure 3.5

Barnum and Bailey's Favorite

Karl L. King
arr. Cathy A. Moklebust

Figure 3.6

B. identify and show an understanding of traditional and handbell and/or handchime music symbols and termnology.

Examples for Meaning:

In the following examples the up-stem ♩ notes are to be played by the right hand and the down-stem ♩ notes are to be played by the left hand.

Level I: Demonstrate the ability to respond to dynamic markings while observing and ringing the accurate duration of note and rest values (see Figure 3.7).

Level II: Show the ability to ring and damp notes and rests accordingly while observing dynamic markings and first and second endings. See also "America" by John Behnke (see Figures 3.8a and 3.8b).

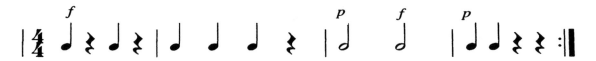

Figure 3.7

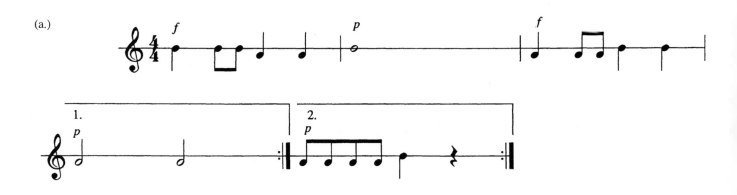

(a.)

(b.) Demonstrates an understanding of the handbells-used chart, tempo and dynamic markings while observing LV, ⊕ and voice lead lines.

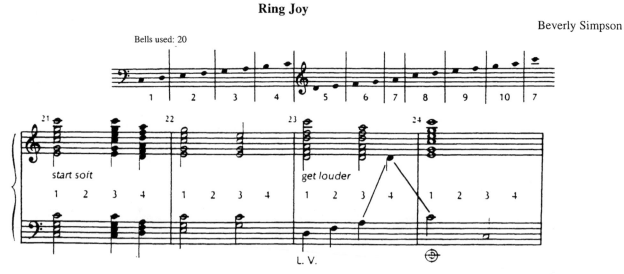

Ring Joy

Beverly Simpson

Figure 3.8

Level III: Ring music scales using different tempos in two or more key signatures while observing dynamics, accents, and fermatas (see Figure 3.9).

Level IV: Demonstrate the ability to musically ring and sight-read more difficult music using multiple key signatures, a wider range of tempos, dynamics, and expression markings (see Figure 3.10).

Level V: Show the ability to perform advanced hand-bell music in a musically appropriate style using all clefs with sudden changes of key signatures, tempos, and expression markings (see Figure 3.11).

(a.)

Down by the Old Millstream

Janet VanValey and Susan Berry

(b.)

Figure 3.9

Guadeamus

Arnold Sherman

Coronation

Kevin McChesney

Figure 3.10

Figure 3.11

Level VI: Demonstrate skilled ability to accurately and expressively interpret and perform Level 5 & 6 handbell music (see Figure 3.12). (Refer to AGEHR difficulty graded levels on a scale 1-6).

C. identify and demonstrate proper execution of traditional notation and handbell and/or handchime music articulation symbols and techniques.

Collage

William Payn

Figure 3.12

Play with R.H. first time, L.H. second time

Figure 3.13

Ballad of Davy Crocket

arr. Martha Lynn Thompson

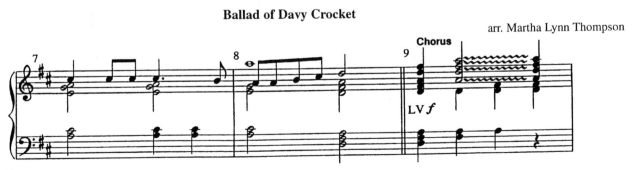

Figure 3.14

Theme from Swedish Rhapsody
(Midsummer Vigil)

Hugo Alfven
arr. Martha Lynn Thompson

Figure 3.15

Examples for Meaning:

Level I: Show the ability to play each note with an appropriate stroke and damp at the end while counting aloud (see Figure 3.13).

Level II: Identify and demonstrate correct usage of sustained sounds indicated by handbell and/or handchime symbols – R, SK, and LV and stopped sound symbols indicated by the staccato dot (see Figure 3.14).

Level III: Identify and demonstrate correct usage of the following sustained sounds indicated by the symbols R, LV, SK, SW, gyro, echo, and vibrato and the following stopped-sound techniques: PL, TD, RT, TPL, BD, table land damp, martellato lift, and mallet.

Caution is to be exercised since not every technique associated with handbells is appropriate with handchimes, especially in stopped-sounds (see Figure 3.15).

Level IV: Demonstrate technical accuracy and control with production of stopped and sustained sounds. See also "This Little Light of Mine" by John Behnke in Appendix G (see Figure 3.16).

Level V: Demonstrate advanced refinement and quick responsiveness to stopped sustained sound handbell and/or handchime techniques (see Figure 3.17).

Level VI: Demonstrate virtuosity in playing all handbell and/or handchime techniques (see Figure 3.18).

Jubilee Hoedown

arr. Kevin McChesney

Figure 3.16

In the Hall of the Mountain King

Edvard Grieg
arr. Michael Keller

Figure 3.17

The Harmonica Player from "Alley Tunes III"

David Guion
arr. Karen Pfiffner

Figure 3.18

Chapter 4

Listening, Responding, Evaluating, and Describing Handbell and/or Handchime Music

Composers and arrangers listen in a finite way to the sounds around them. Great care is given in the choice of instruments for an orchestration, voice color in choral music, and the use of techniques in handbells and handchimes. Sensitive handbell and/or handchime composers understand the impact that each note played by a handbell or handchime has on the final product. They understand which technique should be used in order to maximize the desired effect.

In the grand scheme of composition, there are only three types of literature – original compositions, transcriptions of works for other instruments, and arrangements. Each serves a unique place in the needs of the director/teacher and of the performer. Each also serves a unique place in the mind of the person listening. Arrangements are frequently made of very singable tunes which allow the listener to "hum along" with the melody.

Listening is frequently at the surface level. Transcriptions of orchestral works require the listener to compare the transcription to the original orchestration. While the transcription may stand alone, the mature listener will come to the performance having a knowledge of the original work. Original compositions require the most sophistication on the part of the listener because they have no pre-existing melody as in an arrangement, nor do they have a previous listening experience on which to depend. There is a place for each type of piece in a complete handbell and/or handchime program.

Responding to music is a natural experience. We respond every day – tapping, nodding, whistling, humming, and singing. These are all natural responses, but responding is not necessarily listening. Our society encourages responding to music much more than actually listening. Advertisers know what type of music sells a particular product; movie producers know what style of music to use for particular scenes to gain the desired response.

Since music is around us constantly – in the elevator, shopping center, car radio, television, even on the telephone while we wait – society has taught us to respond instantly and to know when to listen or when to ignore it entirely.

Intellectual and emotional elements are necessary for a complete listening experience. In order to develop the complete listening experience, the listener must understand the organizational structure, have an appropriate emotional response to the appeal of the piece, and allow the piece to impact their senses. As a young child, the goal is to respond in an appropriate manner to the music that surrounds the listener. Teachers ask students to "tap in rhythm," to "move to the beat of the music," to demonstrate when the music is "high" or "low" – all necessary responses to the learning process. As students develop, they move from the physical to the listening mode. This includes both intellectual and emotional responses.

The intellectual level of listening, versus emotional, is an easy place to start since various structural elements of the piece can be easily demonstrated – "raise your hand when we get to the 'B' section" or "raise your hand when you hear the trumpet." Appropriate responses to the emotion and to the senses require a growing maturity on the part of the student. It is at this point that the student can no longer be forced to "listen." The effective director/teacher develops techniques that move the student beyond the intellectual level and involve the student in both levels of listening.

When performing, ringers should be fully involved so they understand what influence they have on the total piece. Ringers need to be constantly reminded to listen to the other ringers. An oboist playing in an orchestra must listen to know how their melody line responds to the earlier bassoon line. A singer must constantly listen and respond appropriately to keep a duet in balance. A handbell and/or handchime ringer must also listen and respond to the notes before and after, as well as the notes that are rung simultaneously. They must understand how their particular note is part of a melody line, part of the harmonic structure, or part of the rhythmic drive of the piece. This is accomplished by developing good listening techniques. It is a disservice to have ringers only follow the directors cue to "ring on beat 3" and then have to keep rehearsing because the ringer keeps pushing the beat or because another ringer is consistently early and the entrance sounds late. The director must begin providing appropriate information so that students might begin providing an appropriate intellectual response. Basic elements of music (form, rhythm, tempo, etc.) and instrumentation are good places to start. How much better it would be to teach a ringer to "listen" so that he or she may respond in an appropriate manner to the musical demands of the piece.

Members of a handbell and/or handchime choir must be given opportunities to respond to the music they are ringing. Analysis of the work must be undertaken on the part of both the director and ringers, with the complexity of the analysis determined by the ringers' ability to respond. When ringers are able to observe that notation is different in different sections of the piece or they observe dynamic contrasts, tempo changes, key changes, etc., they will have the technical means to respond to the music. In some pieces, it would be appropriate to have students describe feelings in various sections. Ringers must be able to respond to their technical problems, i.e., having to ring three bells and handle the necessary changes and be able to solve them. As ringers mature, they will be able to respond appropriately to unity and variety as well as to tension and release in a composition. They should also be able to give examples of similar works — responding, describing and evaluating the music that they have just listened to or rung.

For listening purposes, a random sampling of available recordings can be found at the back of the book in Appendix B.

Chapter 5

Creating Handbell and/or Handchime Music

Students will improvise and create music while using handbells and/or handchimes.

Introduction

Improvise music with handbells and/or handchimes? Impossible you say. Look again. Consider the basis of improvisation and then let individual ringers or groups of ringers add the improvisatory element. Jazz musicians frequently improvise around a recurring chordal pattern or melodic repetition, while elementary music students frequently improvise around a pentatonic scale using either voice or barred instruments. Both groups of musicians also use rhythmic patterns as an integral part of the improvisatory process. By meeting National Standard #3, students will be able to use handbells and/or handchimes with a variety of handbell and/or handchime techniques in an improvisatory manner.

Improvisation

Key Components

In order to meet this standard, students will

* improvise original rhythm patterns while playing handbells and/or handchimes;
* create melodic phrases and songs using handbells and/or handchimes;
* explore and produce various sounds unique to handbells and/or handchimes; and
* experiment with changes in dynamics, texture, form, and meter with handbells and/or handchimes.

Ringers that improvise must understand acoustically what happens in a sound envelope while they are ringing and what it is about acoustics that causes the unique handbell sound. A sound envelope is three basic parts: (1) attack; (2) steady state; (3) decay. Handbells, handchimes, and a very small number of other musical instruments are

unique in the musical world in that they do not possess a discernible steady state. The instant that a handbell and/or handchime is rung, the sound begins to decay. Because of this lack of steady state, ringers and directors have always focused attention on attack and decay. The shake and the trill are used to artificially simulate a steady state, while mallets, plucking, and martellato techniques impact the attack. Decay is affected by various damping techniques (thumb, hand, brush, or table). Some techniques can and do affect both the attack and decay, namely various stopped sounds, martellato, and ring touch. If a ringer fully understands what is happening acoustically with the handbell or handchime when they ring it, a much wider variety of improvisatory techniques become available. The ringer that wants to improvise should spend a great deal of time listening to the sound envelope when they ring various bells. They should go beyond just ringing and begin listening to the attack and decay of every bell that is rung. Listen to what happens when a bell is rung softly versus loudly, how much longer the decay is in a low bell versus a high bell, and how the harmonics change when using mallets on different strike zones of the bell. As bells are listened to, begin combining two bells at a time either harmonically or rhythmically. Experiment and begin replacing one bell with another while continuing the rhythmic pattern – slow at first, faster later. Many techniques mentioned above may be greatly simplified for use with Level I ringers. Bear in mind that only two types of improvisation are possible – melodic and harmonic. Texture/timbre, dynamics, rhythmic patterns, and form can be applied to either melodic or harmonic improvisations.

Examples of Improvisation Techniques

Melodic improvisation can best be learned by imitation. A dialogue approach is in three parts: (1) repeat the pattern exactly as presented; (2) repeat the pattern as presented with change in style (mallets, mart, plucking, etc.);

(3) respond with a totally improvised answer. The director or ringer can use voice, handbells and/or handchimes, a keyboard or other instruments for the original statement.

A director has a multitude of choices for delivery in the handbell rehearsal. If a rhythmic improvisation is to be used, ringers could select one or two handbells or handchimes and all respond at once to the original statement. At the beginning, ringers might clap instead of using handbells or handchimes as a method of responding. For melodic and rhythmic improvisation, directors could also present the same statement over and over asking individuals to respond so that everyone might hear the response (see Figure 5.1).

Once ringers have learned how to improvise the example above, provide an improvisation outline and allow the improvisation to expand. To develop an outline, select a number of ringers that have demonstrated success, and have them ring their improvisation sequentially with a rhythmic pattern between ringers. This could be further expanded by having the other ringers clap the pulse behind the solo ringer and then have them improvise using body percussion (to include clapping) as the next ringer moves

to the bells. An improvisation outline might look something like this:

A   Statement of theme
B   Interlude (clapping of rhythmic pattern)
C   First improvisation
B   Interlude
C   Second improvisation, etc.
D   Tag – this would be a previously practiced ending to the piece, possibly involving two ringers that rang earlier and someone on body percussion.

Learning chord patterns is a simple task and provides a multitude of support for individual or group improvisation. The director has a three-fold responsibility when improvising using chords: (1) build basic chords and chord progressions; (2) select appropriate handbells and/or handchimes within each chord; and (3) apply appropriately voiced chords to various chordal patterns.

First, build a chord on each of the eight steps of the scale (see Figure 5.2).

Train the handbell and/or handchime ensemble to play chords on signal. Using hand signs, indicate the chord by the number of fingers that you hold up. The director must

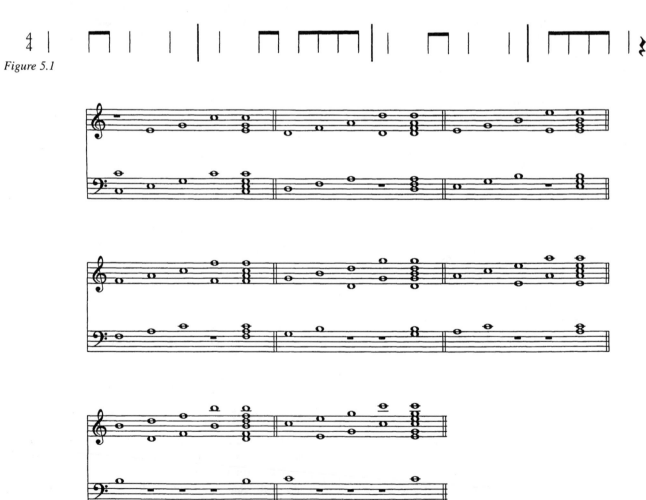

Figure 5.1

Figure 5.2

give enough notice for the ringers to lay down the handbell and/or handchime and pick of the next one needed. If you are playing in a slow four, sign the next chord on beat three. The faster the tempo, the earlier the hand sign.

The simplest chord sequence is I, IV, V, I. Through experimentation, directors will discover that ii, iii, and vi are good substitutes for IV. Using substitutes, here are four additional progressions:

a)	I	vi	IV	V	I
b)	I	iii	IV	V	I
c)	I	ii	IV	V	I
d)	I	vi	ii	V	I

After the handbell and/or handchime choir learns the sequence, incorporate rhythmic alternatives (see Figure 5.3).

As choirs develop skills, they might want to add pass-ing notes between chords (see Figure 5.4).

The cornerstone of jazz improvisation is the Blues Progression. Having been used in all periods and styles of jazz, this serves as the basis for jazz accompaniment patterns. It is a 12-measure sequence using the following chords (see Figure 5.5). Try:

- ringing the pattern with a variety of rhythms and techniques (see Figure 5.6);
- ringing the pattern in triple meter rather than duple meter and using complex meters and mixed meters;
- "pushing" chords ahead of the beat for a little rhythmic accent;
- using a "lag-a-long" style where, like the opposite of "pushing," you delay the arrival of the chord by an infinitesimal amount of time;

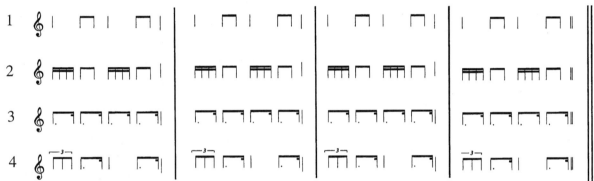

Figure 5.3

Figure 5.4   I   vi   IV   V   I   I   vi   IV   V   I

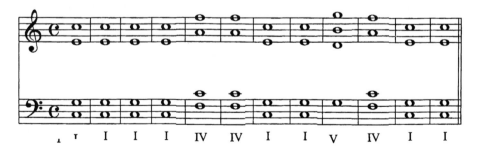

Figure 5.5   I   I   I   I   IV   IV   I   I   V   IV   I   I

Figure 5.6

- accenting the second and fourth beat of the measure;
- arpeggios of the chord throughout the measure – both bottom to top and top to bottom;
- adding nonchordal notes ahead of the beat, i.e., E-flat into an E in a C chord;
- improvising in other keys (just play up the scale developing a chord on each scale note);
- improvising above a drone bass line that is either static or has a rhythmic pattern;
- substituting a V7 chord for a V chord.

As directors and ringers learn to improvise, more and more options for improvisation will present themselves.

- Develop a simple whole or half note exercise and teach it to the handbell and/or handchime choir. As you listen to handbells and handchimes, instruct students to change from ringing to shaking, tower swings and other techniques. Increase the speed and add thumb damps, marts, plucks, or ring touches.
- When you develop the exercise, consider the form of the piece:
  - Verse/Refrain – Teach the choir a prewritten refrain of four or eight measures, and allow one or two assigned ringers to improvise the verse.
  - Rondo – Develop a four-bar melody to act as section A; assign ringers four bars in which to improvise with their two bells on various rhythms, pitches, and techniques.
  - Canon – Use as a form for a modified improvisation. Select an existing canon and allow ringers to experiment with various entrances, octaves, and techniques.
- In a piece that has been previously learned, have students experiment with changes in dynamics from what the composer or editor has published.
- Select a simple song in four and, on a certain measure, change to three or five. The resulting accent will encourage further improvisation.

- Allow a student to use a single handbell/handchime to develop an eight-beat rhythmic pattern.

At the end of the pattern, the student points to another ringer who "answers" the eight-beat statement. As students grow in ability, add a second or third bell or chime and allow students to add additional handbell or handchime techniques.

- Select a major, minor or modal scale. Develop a peal with pitches and then improvise a vocal or instrumental melody over the peal.
- Write a ground bass. Allow students to use higher bells or chimes to improvise a short one to four measure improvisation on top of the ground bass.

A more complex and different style of improvisation involving aleatory operations was developed by Everett Jay Hilty (Professor Emeritus, University of Colorado at Boulder) quite a few years ago. He composed a series of three-note rhythmic compositions that could be played together in any number of combinations, depending on the number of ringers available. Ringers were instructed to select a low, middle, and high bell and to ring in conjunction with other ringers. Dynamic ranges, tempos, and a whole host of other decisions must be made by the director. One of the most important choices is whether in subsequent performances ringers will be allowed to let chance operation (aleatory) determine the outcome of the piece, or whether during rehearsal, predetermined handbells and/or handchimes will be used. While this type of piece is very structured, leaving little choice for the individual player, the director is in total control of the aleatoric operations and thus in control of the improvisational aspect of the piece. The overall shape of the piece will be determined as ringers are added and subtracted. If a director chooses to compose a series of three-note rhythmic compositions, they should be eight or sixteen measures in length and similar in rhythmic difficulty. The complexity of the rhythms will happen as parts are played together (see Figure 5.7).

Ringer

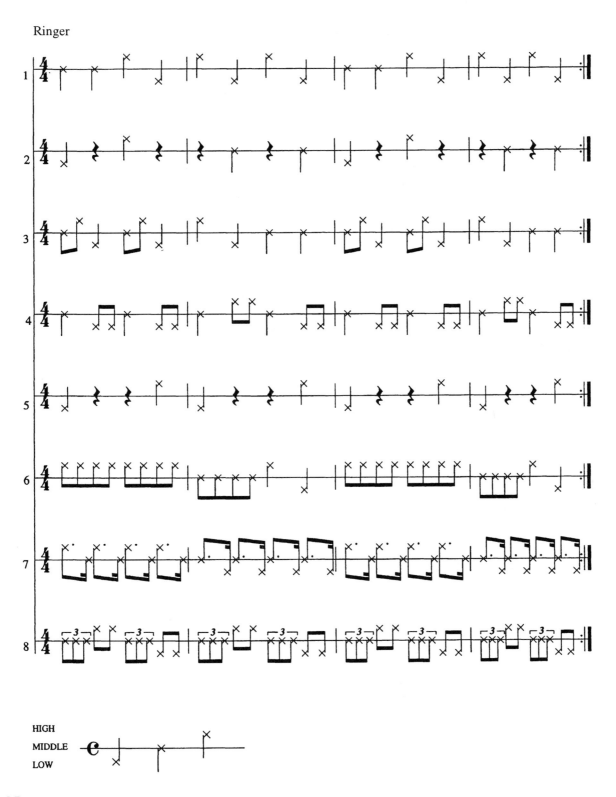

Figure 5.7

"Music produces a kind of pleasure which human nature cannot do without."
— Confucious

Chapter 6

Understanding Music and the Role of Handbells and/or Handchimes

The arts lie deep in human nature, where they reflect society. Children, both in and out of the classroom, use all the arts by making up stories, creating art on the sidewalk, dancing, and creating songs. They spontaneously create with limited knowledge of form, style, historical perspective, etc. As children grow, society expects their creative efforts to be more complex and to be more specialized. Society expects adults to write out the stories that they created in their heads, turn in their chalk and replace it with oils and acrylics, organize dance projects around a theme, and place the music on manuscript paper so that others might perform the music. Adults become much more aware of the audience and feel they must create their works for them rather than for their childhood self-satisfaction or peer approval.

While responding to music is natural and requires no formal understanding of the art form, participants in music must understand the technical requirements necessary. They also need to understand their role as a participant. Students, be they young or old, use a variety of means for educating themselves about the arts. They experience performance as a listener, learn to play an instrument, sing in a choir, create music in the classroom, take music theory/appreciation/history classes, join a handbell and/or handchime choir, or simply listen to the music around them. For the majority of individuals, formalized instruction in music is to further one's personal enjoyment.

Since it is experienced on different levels, music is much easier to experience than to define. Sometimes the experience is to entertain while other times it is to extract emotions from the audience. Tolstoi said it best: "Art is a human activity having for its purpose the transmission to others of the highest and best feelings to which man has risen."

When it comes to creating or performing music, the twentieth century has afforded us a plethora of options. For the first time in musical history, there is a strong desire to research and authentically recreate the music of earlier composers. In reviewing various periods in music history, change came about because society felt that the previous musical period no longer reflected the needs of the contemporaneous society. Because of our contemporary interest in recreating historical music, we are afforded not only music from various historical periods, but also a much wider variety of ethnic and cultural choices. For example, a composition might use an identifiable ethnic rhythm to support a newly written melody that is reminiscent of a totally different culture and the audience supports it with applause. Likewise, twentieth-century composers use past compositions as the basis of newly created works.

Historically, handbell ringing can be traced back to the British Isles in the early days of Christianity, with small bells without handles or clappers appearing between the eleventh and sixteenth centuries. Medieval manuscripts from that time show music in two-part harmony.

"Up to the sixteenth century all bellringing in England had been done in the church towers, and the ringing consisted of the strange and wonderful art of 'ringing the changes' – the changes being a series of ever-changing patterns, no two being repeated, and following cruelly complex rules, well established by the mid-seventeenth century. Patterns of changes are not repeated from start (a downward scale) to finish (return to the downward scale)."

Imagine this: a band of ringers standing in a circle facing each other in a cold and drafty tower. Each ringer holds a rope that goes through a hole in the ceiling above them, winding around a wheel assembly stationed on the floor. A good hefty pull on the rope turns the wheel which rotates the bell, one for every ringer. Teams of ringers would "ring the changes" by following a mathematical series for which they had memorized a prescribed set of rules. These sets of permutations sometimes took hours to complete, depending on the number of bells and the type of ring. Such patterns were called by some rather colorful names such as Plain Bob, Reverse Canterbury Bob, Kent Treble Bob, and Plain Hunt.

Short and simple rings for three, four, or five bells might look something like this:

For Three Bells	**For Four Bells**	**For Five Bells**
1 2 3	1 2 3 4	1 2 3 4 5
1 3 2	2 1 4 3	1 3 2 5 4
3 1 2	2 4 1 3	3 1 5 2 4
3 2 1	4 2 3 1	3 5 1 4 2
2 3 1	4 3 2 1	5 3 4 1 2
2 1 3	3 4 1 2	5 4 3 2 1
1 2 3	3 1 4 2	4 5 2 3 1
	1 3 2 4	4 2 5 1 3
	1 2 3 4	2 4 1 5 3
		2 1 4 3 5
		1 2 3 4 5

Figure 6.1

Imagine you're ringing the number ten bell in a very long complicated peal. It would be difficult indeed to remember when it's your turn each time round! Notice from the above diagram that each ring ends the same way it began, with the bells being rung in the same order as at the first. If a change starts with 1 2 3 4, it will also end with 1 2 3 4. There is pleasure in the return.

"Change-ringing took a great deal of practicing, and made a great deal of prolonged noise, of which the good people of the neighborhood becomes understandably tired."

Handbell ringing actually began as a less strenuous way of practicing change ringing. With small handbells, the ringers could practice their changes in front of a warm fireplace without disturbing the entire village.

"After the restoration of the Monarchy in 1660, change ringing developed rapidly. Such was the demand for handbells at the end of the century that improved methods of casting were sought, and the Wiltshire bellfoundry, then owned by William and Robert Corr, invented a method of casting handbells in sand moulds."

Evidence of a highly developed technique in the art of change ringing on handbells was witnessed in 1732 when members of the Ancient Society of College Youths presented a concert in Calais, ringing a course of *cinques*.

In 1923, Margaret Shurcliff of Boston, Massachusetts, organized a group of handbell ringers called The Beacon Hill Ringers. Mrs. Shurcliff's influence led to the formation of numerous ringing groups throughout New England and to the formation of the New England Guild of Handbell Ringers in 1937. Handbells were introduced into churches and schools in the late 1940s, thus beginning institutional ownership of handbells. AGEHR was formed in 1954 with Margaret Shurcliff as the Guild's first president.[1]

Handbells and handchimes have been introduced to schools in a much slower manner than in churches. In surveying school districts throughout the country, handbells and/or handchimes have usually been introduced at the insistence of an individual or small group of people. In years past, handchimes were found more frequently in elementary schools, while handbells were more often found in secondary schools. Larger school districts frequently have "traveling" handbell sets that are used by multiple schools for a limited period of time. After using the "traveling" handbells for a few years, individual schools will frequently purchase their own set. As a result, we are now seeing more sets of handbells and/or handchimes in elementary schools.

Because of staffing ratios and the limited number of ringers in a handbell choir, most handbell and/or handchime choirs do not meet during the school day, but meet before school, after school, or during lunch, with performances frequently part of an instrumental or choral performance. In reviewing handbell and/or handchime programs in our schools, existing programs are almost always directed by a strongly motivated individual that sees the use of handbells and handchimes as an effective means of providing a comprehensive music education program that meets the needs of individual students.

1. Frazier, James, Kermit Junkert, Donald Shier, Robert Strusinski, Bonita Wurscher. *Handbells in the Liturgy.* St. Louis: Concordia Publishing House, 1994.

Chapter 7

Assessment

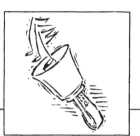

As part of a broad national education reform, the National Standards for Education in the Arts are a voluntary set of standards describing what every child should know and be able to do. The arts are stated as equal partners in the process of the development of standards with other core subject areas. Throughout, the focus is on academic performance and achievement. The Music Standards, as published in this book, define the fundamental principles of what is important in learning to play a handbell or handchime.

The development of handbell and/or handchime expectations, or standards, and benchmarks follows when there is a thorough understanding of the essential competencies and skills to be learned in a sequential framework of instruction for learning how to play handbells and/or handchimes. An important part of this comprehensive course of study is the evaluation of the student's growth, ringing skills, knowledge, and understanding. Directors/teachers have the responsibility to precisely match or align the curriculum, instruction, assessment, and standard to increase the probability that students will be able to meet or exceed the standard. Directors/teachers must also consider the prerequisite skills and knowledge that students should possess before they can learn something new. Various instructional strategies may be used by the teacher to engage the students in learning how to play handbells and/or handchimes such as drill, application, modeling, practice, direct instruction, and performance. Great care should be taken in allowing each student to grow according to his or her personal circumstances. A standards-based organizer can be of great help to the director/teacher (see Figure 7.1).

Assessment is a broad term that refers to the process of gathering and synthesizing information to understand and describe the growth that has occurred. The rationale of assessment is to monitor and guide student learning, not simply to measure it. Continuous assessment:

- informs instruction, tells about students as learners;
- is multi-faceted, is formal or informal;
- appears in a variety of formats;
- is a check for the director/teacher to see if instruction is on target;
- changes depending on the developmental level of the learners;
- is process and product;
- provides a body of evidence;
- needs to be planned and sequenced carefully;
- should provide immediate feedback;
- measures what students need to know and be able to do.

A clear statement of what each student is expected to know is one of the first steps to be taken in order to achieve alignment with the standard. Think of the end result first!

Key questions to ask when planning assessment strategies are:

- What do I want students to know, understand, and be able to do?
- What and why am I assessing?
- How will the information be used, and for whom are the assessment results intended?

The director/teacher designs the assessment on the desired outcome or expectation of a specific content standard. When the evaluative criterion is made explicit in advance, it can serve as a focus for both instruction and evaluation. It is this criterion for quality that effective teachers help their students understand. Teachers provide regular feedback to the students based on identified criterion in addition to peer- and self-evaluation. It is a wise teacher who trains his or her students to be accountable and evaluate themselves. Assessment practices can be

National Arts Standards	Class Handbell Unit Standards	School District Music Standards
Standards #1 2 5 6 7 8 9	Standards #1 2 3	Standards #1 2 4

Vocabulary

   treble clef; bass clef
   whole, half, quarter and eight
    notes and rests
   scale
   sharp, flat, accidental
   handbell, handchime
   bells - used chart
   time signature
   key signature
   ring and damp
   strikepoint
   collar, clapper, handle
   L.V., shake, pluck, T.D.
   moderato

Fifth Grade Handbell Unit

Skills

1. Correct ringing position
2. Damping
3. Read letter names of treble & bass clefs
4. "Connect" letter name of a note on a staff with the size, sound and position of bell when placed in chromatic order
5. Apply note values and rests (whole, half, etc.) to ringing duration
6. Correct execution of basic bell ringing techniques: ring, damp, L.V., shake, pluck, thumb damp

Resources

1. *Ringing For the First Time:* McKechnie Flammer #HL 5232

2. *Time to Ring* arr. Thompson Agape #1873

3. *Clapper Classics* Thompson & Callahan Agape #1254

Strategies

1. Mini-lessons with application
2. Review and practice
3. Demonstrations - small groups
4. Modeling - teacher & student
5. Observation
6. Whole class ringing
7. Overhead transparencies
8. Paper & pencil activities
9. Individual "white board" and dry marker activities
10. Class performance

Assessments

1. Teacher observation pre and post
2. Self-evaluation
3. Small group observation
4. Completion of written evaluation form
5. Venn diagram
6. Question and answer
7. Student performance

Figure 7.1

formal or informal and should include a variety of forms so the student can demonstrate what he or she has learned. For the handbell and/or handchime ringer this may include:

- teacher observation – formative assessment of student readiness (pre)
- self-assessment – students reflect on their own learning
- peer evaluation
- verbal
- attitude and behavior
- participation and attendance
- videotape
- demonstration
- cooperative group assessment
- family and organization observation
- checklists
- written work – note and rhythm reading
- performance
- teacher observation – summative assessment (post).

When assessing, it is imperative that the language used be consistent with the language used during instruction. The director/teacher must carefully identify the skills or content to be assessed and then test only what has been taught. Ask, "What are the observable actions that demonstrate the learning?"

In the following examples a set of scoring and instructional guidelines are used to measure student understanding and achievement. Viewed before performing a task, rubrics define the levels of performance and show students what they need to do to meet or exceed the expected standard for the assignment. School systems across the country use various reporting means to show grades or scores. This book uses 4, 3, 2, 1.

A4 means that the standard has been exceeded. Highest proficiency of the specified knowledge or skill has been achieved.

A3 denotes that the expectation of the standard has been met.

A2 is below standard, and means that the level of skill demonstrated or knowledge shown needs further work or study in order to be accurate. It can be said that the student is moving toward the standard or is "in progress."

A1 shows reason for concern or unsatisfactory performance. A great deal of time or experience is needed by the student in order to grasp the meaning and application of a musical concept and/or handbell and/or handchime playing skill and technique. The student is not showing effort and/or progress appropriate for his or her ability at this time.

If the student receives a 2 or 1, the director/teacher should facilitate a discussion with the student and/or family to formulate interventions which support student learning. Education is a partnership between teachers, students, and parents. Adaptations or changes may be made in the environment, curriculum, or instruction in order for the student to review or perhaps return to a place where he or she can be successful. Teachers then continue to monitor and adjust as new skills and understandings are built. When assessing the ringer, it goes without saying that the student needs to be comfortable and in a physical environment where he or she feels it's okay to take risks. In other words, consideration should be given for a familiar bell assignment, as well as the bell manufacturer, table height, room lighting, and outside noise control. It behooves the teacher to generate a positive attitude and to create a congenial learning atmosphere.

Figure 7.2

Following is an example showing the expectation of a specified task and rubrics developed to evaluate a Level II, Advanced Beginner B4, C5 ringer's ability, and knowledge in maintaining a steady tempo.

Prerequisite skills and knowledge could include such things as:

- mental development (language and reading ability)
- physical strength and coordination
- music readiness and achievement
- interest of student and his or her support system (Cultural; level of work ethic; development of dedication and commitment; attendance and punctuality)
- handbell and/or handchime playing experience (Performance energy, charisma and communication with audience; development of sensitive listening and hearing)

Standard: The B4, C5 ringer will accurately play the B4, C5 playing position while maintaining a steady tempo (see Figure 7.2).

Example of rubrics for Level II (Advanced Beginner) ringer:

4   The ringer exceeds the standard accurately and precisely rings and damps the B4, C5 playing position with correct rhythm and tempo while making bell and/or chime changes with ease and confidence.

3   The ringer meets the standard accurately and precisely rings and damps the B4, C5 playing position with correct rhythm and tempo while making bell and/or chime changes.

2   The ringer was unable to maintain a steady tempo either because of bell changes, lack of rhythmic accuracy or precision in attack and release of bell and/or chime tone, and/or did not pick up and put down assigned bells with ease and confidence.

1   The ringer was unable to maintain a steady tempo, had inaccuracies of note and rest values, and had difficulty in making bell changes.

Of course, other qualities could be assessed in this example, such as the dynamics, the matching of tones, performance style, etc. It is essential to be very specific about what is being observed and not "overload" the young student by expecting too much at one time. As a ringer's knowledge and skill increases, the criterion can become even more specific and challenging, all done in the spirit of encouraging growth and achievement. The evaluation of an Advanced (Level V) ringer can greatly differ from that of a Level II ringer. In the following example, the specific criterion for the B4, C5 ringer is focused on ringing musically while maintaining the tempo.

Standard: The ringer will accurately and musically play the B4, C5 position while maintaining a steady tempo (see Figure 7.3).

Figure 7.3

Example of rubrics for the Level V (Advanced) ringer:

4   The ringer exceeds the standard by demonstrating high proficiency in maintaining steady tempo while playing with skilled musicality.

3   The ringer meets the standard while accurately maintaining the tempo while playing musically.

2   The ringer had some difficulty in keeping the tempo and/or playing musically.

1   The ringer had great difficulty in maintaining a steady tempo and/or playing musically.

Following are additional ideas for assessment of handbell skills and achievement:

- a student-developed evaluation form that allows each member of the class/ensemble to have input on the quality of a performance and provides each with clear information as to areas where improvement is needed (see Figure 7.4).
- a jointly developed (teacher and students) collection and comparison of information on two performances, two selections of music; or two rehearsals in the form of a Venn diagram.

Specific information of each is entered in each of the outside circles of the Venn diagram.

Common information is entered in the intersection of

Example of a student-developed evaluation on the quality of a performance.

Ringer's Name _____ Date _____

Handbell Playing Position _____

"Spring Concert" _____ School _____

Check level of achievement for each category:	4 (above)	3 (standard)	2 (below)	1 (way below)	Plan of action for improvement
1. Note Accuracy					
2. Rhythm Accuracy					
3. Tempo Accuracy (steady beat, changes)					
4. Musicality (dynamics, voicing)					
5. Technique Accuracy					
6. Watch and Listen to Director					
7. Teamwork and Responsibility					
8. Stage Presence					

Figure 7.4

the two circles with discussion leading to in-depth evaluation of the music and handbell playing (see Figure 7.5).

The assessment program is intended to directly impact student learning, as well as provide data for student growth. It is a continuous process and, as previously mentioned, can take varied forms. However, teacher observation using specified criterion will be one of the most useful since the art of handbell and/or handchime ringing is visual and audible, as well as physical and uniquely expressive. Some of what the director or teacher chooses to critique may be determined ahead of time but, more likely, spontaneous judgments during rehearsal will be made on such things as correct notes being played, balance of dynamics or tone production, articulation and rhythmic precision. It's important that the assessment matches what has been taught.

The standards support accountability toward an advanced level of achievement for educators, teachers, and students. Every director/teacher must ask, "What is it that I want my students to know and be able to do?" The answer to those questions determines the assessment criterion. Driven by the assessment, instruction and curriculum are developed to focus on the teaching of the key points of the standards and benchmarks.

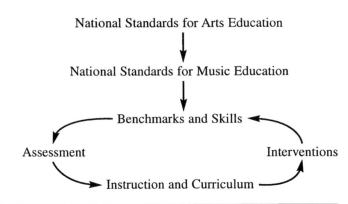

Collection and comparison of handbell choir members' memorization of last two measures of "Sarasponda," page 61, measures 39 and 40 and "Variations on a French Tune," page 45, measures 35 and 36.

"Ringing for the First Time" by D. Linda McKechnie Flammer, #HL 52 32

Directions: Place your playing position number (i.e., C4, D4 = playing position #1) in the appropriate area of the Venn diagram to correspond to which music selections the last two measures are memorized.

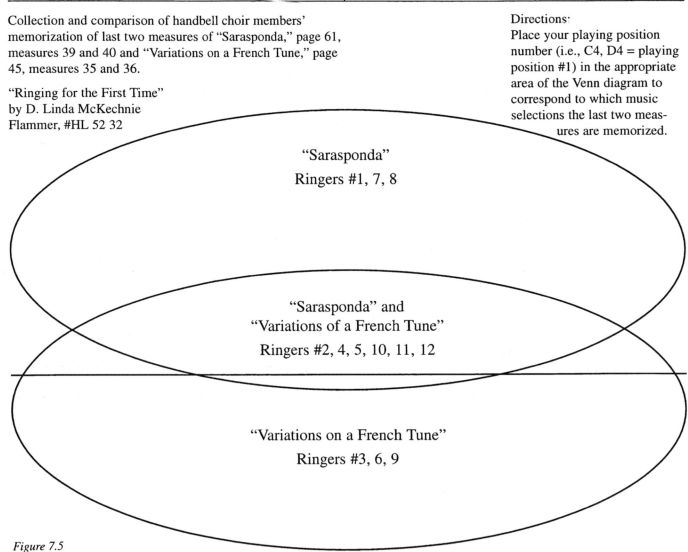

"Sarasponda" Ringers #1, 7, 8

"Sarasponda" and "Variations of a French Tune" Ringers #2, 4, 5, 10, 11, 12

"Variations on a French Tune" Ringers #3, 6, 9

Figure 7.5

Summary

In accepting the National Standards for Arts Education, Secretary of Education Richard Riley stated that "these voluntary standards should be a welcome resource for concerned state and local educators, parents, and communities who are interested in giving their children . . . a rigorous, sequential study of the four arts disciplines. The process of studying and creating art in all of its distinct forms defines . . . those qualities that are at the heart of education reform – creativity, perseverance, a sense of standards, and above all, a striving for excellence."

If you have read all the ideas and suggestions contained in this book, the rationale for inclusion of handbells and handchimes in a music education program as a means of meeting the National Standards in Music Education now exists. According to the most recent National Education Goals Panel (NAGP) Annual Report, at least thirty-two states have developed sets of education standards and another fourteen have standards in development. While some of the thirty-two states and some local districts have chosen to call them something other than standards, the goal is the same – to help children, parents, educators, and the community to realize the value and importance of music in our society today.

In applying the Standards, as stated in this publication, to your local handbell and/or handchime program, modify the content of the various chapters to your local situation and, as you develop your program, keep the Standards foremost in your planning process. If done properly, handbells and handchimes will help cultivate the whole child.

Appendix A

Suggested Literature List

Title	Composer/Arranger	Octaves	Publisher	Code
LEVEL 1				
Earth & All Stars	David Johnson/Shepard	3/5	Hinshaw Music Inc.	HHB 37
Entrata & Exuberance	Margaret Tucker	2/3	Alfred	#12411
Processional Alleluia	Kevin McChesney	3-4 opt brass	Jeffers	JHS9191B
Processional Alleluia	Kevin McChesney	3-4 opt brass	Jeffers	JHS9191FS
There's a Little Wheel A-Turnin'	arr. England & Sherman		Ring Out Press	RO2702
Ring Together Children's Songs	arr. Kevin McChesney	2/3	Jeffers	JH S9240
Morning Song	Kevin McChesney	2/3	Ringing Word	RW 8097
Three American Melodies	arr. Jay Althouse	2	Alfred	8657
Two Fanfares for Bells	Michael R. Keller	2/3	Alfred	16474
Bellsong	Douglas Wagner	2	Lorenz	LZ-20/1152L
Carillon Celebration	Douglas Wagner	3	Lorenz	LZ-20/1114L
Fanfare	Mussorgsky/Sherman	3,4,5	Jeffers	JHS-9151
Huron Carol	Waugh	3	Jeffers	JHS-9181
Jingle Bells	Kevin McChesney	2,3	Genesis Press	GP-1019
Jolly Old St. Nicholas	Cynthia Dobrinski	2,3	Genesis Press	GP-1006
Ode to Joy	Beethoven/Maggs	3	Genesis Press	GP-1002
Scarborough Fair	Maggs	3	Genesis Press	GP-1018
Shenandoah	Sue Ellen Page	2,3	Alfred	AF 16478
LEVEL 2				
Two American Folk Songs	arr. Valerie Stephenson	2/3	Jeffers	JH S9168
With Timbrel & Dance	Margaret R. Tucker	3 opt inst	Composers Music Co.	BE 0436
Land of the Silver Birch	arr. Patricia A. Thomson	3/5	AGEHR	AG35129
Suite for Handbells	Michael Helman	2/3	AGEHR	AG23008
Sakura Melody Fanfare	arr. Katsumi Kodama	4	AGEHR	AG 4035
DeColores	William Wood	3/5	Jeffers	JH S9210
London Bells	arr. Sandra Winter	3/5	Handbell Ringers of GB	35/04
Mallet Madness	Kirtsy Mitchell	3/5	AGEHR	AG35106
My Favorite Things	Rodgers/Hammerstein, arr. Douglas E. Wagner	3/5	Agape	1609
Scarborough Fair	arr. Paul A. McKleveen	3/5	Alfred	12413
Allegro In C	Mozart/McChesney	2+	AGEHR	AG-3076
An American Fantasy	Moklebust	2	Posthorn Press	POS-B1035
Andante Maestoso	Holst/McChesney	2	Beckenhorst Press	BH-HB 180A
Bells of Notre Dame	Menken/Stephenson	2	Jeffers	JHS-9223
English Folk Song	Everett Jay Hilty	2	Flagstaff Publishing	FPC-HB 132
Evening Song	Duvemoy/Luethi	2	Flagstaff Publishing	FPC-HB 135

Fantasy on a French Carol	Hal Hopson	2	Ringing Word Press	RW-8105
Kolyada	Waugh	2	Jeffers	JHS-9196
Little Minuet	Bach/McChesney	2	Jeffers	JHS-9197
Little Prelude	Bach/McChesney	2	Jeffers	JHS-9172
Prelude in D	Bach/Luethi	2	Flagstaff Publishing	FPC-HB 145
Red River Valley	Merrett	2	Flagstaff Publishing	FPC-HB 165
Ring Around a Rainbow	Kinyon	2	Alfred	AF-17550
Rondo	Tucker	2	Concordia Publishing	CPH97-6406
Simple Santa	Hakes	2	Ring Out Press	RO 3201
Sonatina No. 1	Helman	3,4,5	AGEHR	AG 35153
Songs of America	Doug Wagner	2	National Music	NMP-137
Star Spangled Banner	Key/Bartsch	2	Jeffers	JHS-9040P
Yankee Doodle	Mitchell	3,4,5	AGEHR	AG-35114
Alleluia	Hentz	2,3,4	Bel Canto	

LEVEL 3

Resonance & Reflection	Margaret R. Tucker	3-5 opt inst.	Alfred	17552
Jubilee for Bells	Barbara Kinyon	4/5	Agape	1713
Nocturne in E minor	Cynthia Dobrinski	4/5	Agape	498
Prelude in Classic Style	Gordon Young, arr. Tammy Waldrop	5 (opt 6-7)	Lorenz	20/11102
Battle Hymn of the Republic	arr. Cynthia Dobrinski	3-5 opt inst.	Agape	1862
Fantasy No. 1 in F minor	Arnold B. Sherman	3/5	Agape	1698
Allegro #4 from Royal Fireworks Music	Handel/Baker	3	Bronze FX	BFX-004
Alotta Staccata	Waldrop	2,3	Lorenz	LZ-20/1155L
America the Beautiful	Ward/Sherman	3,4,5,6	Red River Press	RR-FS0002
Andante from Water Music	Handel/McChesney	3,4,5	Flagstaff Publishing	FPC-HB163
Arab Dance	Tchaikovsky/McChesney	3,4,5	Jeffers	JHS-9246
Bell Boogie	Smith	3,4	Red River Press	RR-BL5014
Deck the Halls	Kevin McChesney	3,4	Hope Publishing	HP-2060
Good King Wenceslas	Hart Morris	3,4,5	Alfred	AF-12412
Holly and the Ivy, The	Kevin McChesney	3,4,5	Ringing Word	RW-8100 FS
I Saw Three Ships	Rogers	3	Jeffers	JHS-9201
Jingle Bells	Bock/Mathis	2,3	Fred Bock Music	FB-BG0946
Kiss the Girl	Menken/McChesney	3,4,5	Jeffers	JHS-9215
Moon Over the Ruined Castle	Taki/Anraku	3,4,5	AGEHR	AG-35105
Nutcracker, The	Tchaikovsky/McChesney	3,4,5	Lorenz	LZ-20/1078L
Siyahamba-African Freedom Song	Ward	4,5,6	AGEHR	AG 46014
Song of the Bells	Mozart/Downey	3,4,5	AGEHR	AG 35137
Trepak	Tchaikovsky/Merrett	3,4	Hope Publishing	HP-1330
Virginia Highlands Suite	Cynthia Dobrinski	3,4,5	Hope Publishing	HP-1886

LEVEL 4

A Classical Ring	Valerie W. Stephenson	3/5	Lorenz	20/1128L
Spiritdance	Sondra K. Tucker	3/5	Concordia	97-6711
Suo Gan	arr. Jeffery A. Hall	3 to 6	Alfred	17536
The All American Hometown Band	arr. William R. Wood	4/5	AGEHR	45019
The Billboard March	arr. Mary Kay Parrish	4/5	Agape	1778
Cascades	Karen Buckwalter	3 to 6	Harold Flammer	HP 5351
Rondo-Passacaglia	Cynthia Dobrinski	4/5	Agape	1237
Dr. Martin Luther King, Jr. Tribute	Laurence	5,6	AGEHR	AG 56006J
Easy Winners, The	Joplin/McChesney	3,4,5	Fred Bock Press	FB-JG0714
Entertainer, The	Joplin/Roger	3,4,5	Jeffers	JHS-9183
Fantasy	Helman	3,4,5	AGEHR	AG-35117
Festive Dance	Bizet/McChesney	3,4,5,6,7	Jeffers	JHS-9195
Gladiolus Rag	Joplin/Allen	3,4,5	BronzeFX	BFX-009
Gypsy Dance	Kevin McChesney	3,4,5	AGEHR	AG-35073
Humoresque	Dvorak/Wilson	2	Flagstaff Publishing	FPC HB162
Italian Sailors Song	Shumann/Hilty	4	Flagstaff Publishing	FPC HB121
Jubilee Hoedown	Kevin McChesney	3,4,5	AGEHR	AG-35098
Kaleidoscope	Luethi	4	Flagstaff Publishing	FPC-HB119

New Pizzicato Polka	Strauss/Thompson	3,4,5	AGEHR	AG 35132
Nocturne in C minor	Helman	3,4,5	AGEHR	AG 35120
Pick a Winner	Gillis	4	AGEHR	AG-4030
Polka Fest	Karen Buckwalter	3,4,5	AGEHR	AG-35133
Rondo Alla Turca	Mozart/Meredith	5,6	Meredith Music Pub	MMP-9805
Scherzo	Everett Jay Hilty	2	Flagstaff Publishing	FPC HB152
Skip to My Lou	Kinyon	3,4,5	Hope (Agape)	HP 1929
When Johnny Comes Marching Home	Stephenson	3,4,5,6	Hope (Agape)	HP 1903

LEVEL 5

Danse Arabe	arr. William H. Griffin	4-6HB/3-4HC	Beckenhorst	HB176
Can-Can	Rossini, arr. Phillip M. Young	4/5	AGEHR	AG45-44
Dance of the Reed Flutes	Tchaikowsky, arr. Jefferey A. Hall	4/5	Alfred	16464
Elegy	William A. Payn	4/5	Agape	1277
March from "The Love of Three Oranges"	Prokofieff, arr. Arnold B. Sherman	4 to 6	AGEHR	AG 46005
Villancico	arr. Gail Downey	3-5 (opt 2-3 HC)	National	HB438
Reflections	Betty Garee	5	Harold Flammer	HP 5078
Adagio and Toccata	Frescobaldi/Kangas	4,5,6,7	Bell Canto Press	BCP BCC1
From the New World Symphony No. 9 - 3rd Movement	Dvorak/Baker	4,5,6	AGEHR	AG 46006
Great Gate of Kiev, The	Mourssorgsky/Thompson	4,5,6	AGEHR	AG-46006
Introduction and Passacaglia	Margaret Tucker	5,6,7	AGEHR	AG-57003
Lonesome Valley	Hart Morris	3,4,5	Beckenhorst	BH-HB155
Marche from the Nutcracker	Tchaikovsky/Griffin	5,6,7	AGEHR	AG 57007J
Marche Miniature	Tchaikovsky/Young	3,4,5	National	NMP-HB428
Night at the Opera, A	Laurence	4,5,6	AGEHR	AG-46013
Nocturne No. 3	Liszt/Muschick	5, 6	AGEHR	AG-56005
Norwegian Dance	Grieg/Stephenson	4,5,6,7	AGEHR	AG 47001
Perpetual Motion	Don Allured	4	National	NMP-HB447
Overture	Handel/Meredith	4,5,6	Meredith Music Pub	MMP-9814
Overture from the Barber of Seville	Rossini/Thompson	4,5,6	Jeffers	JHS-9229
Russian Dance	Gliere/Griffin	4,5,6,7	Jeffers	JHS-9236
Scherzo in A minor	Karen Buckwalter	3,4,5	AGEHR	AG-35147
Take Five	Desmond/Campanile	5	Laurendale Assoc.	LD-HB1045
Up On the Housetop	Sherman	3,4,5,6	Hope (Agape)	HP 2055
We Wish You a Ragtime Christmas	Campanile	5	Laurendale Assoc.	LD-HB1053

LEVEL 6

Four Prelude	Shostakovich, arr. Everett Jay Hilty	6	Flagstaff	HB 186
Consecration	William A. Payn	5 (opt 2 oct HC)	Agape	1933
Transfiguration	Michael R. Keller	5/7	AGEHR	AG57002
Uncommon Adoration	Hart Morris	5/6	AGEHR	AG56004
Holiday for Strings	Rose/Homibrook	3,4	Shawnee Press	SP HP 5085
Kaminnoi-Ostrow	Rubinstein/Hilty	4,5	Flagstaff	FPC HB123
La Zingana	Bohm/Pfiffner	4,5	Flagstaff	FPC HB196
Leyenda	Albeniz/Meredith	5,6	Meredith Music Pub	MMP 9801
Rondalla Argonessa	Grandas/Pfiffner	5	Flagstaff	FPC-HB155
Blue Rondo a la Turk	Brubeck/Benton/Thorneycroft	5/6	Beckenhorst Press	HB77
Antiphonal Alleluias	Hart Morris	5,6,7	AGEHR	AG57006J
Scherzo in A minor	Karen Lakey Buckwalter	3,4,5	AGEHR	AG35147

Appendix B

Technique/Skills

Title	Composer/Arranger	Octaves	Publisher	Code
Successful Ringing: Step by Step	John A. Behnke	2/3/4/5	CPH - Concordia	99/1678
Time to Ring	Martha L. Thompson	1/2	Agape	1873
Five Easy Celebrations	Michael R. Keller	3/5	Agape	1615
Mousterpieces	arr. Martha L. Thompson	3	Hal Leonard	
Begin to Ring	Martha L. Thompson/Frances L. Callahan	3	Agape	1243
Begin to Ring	Martha L. Thompson/Frances L. Callahan	2	Agape	1242
Ready to Ring	Martha L. Thompson/Frances L. Callahan	2/5	Agape	1110
Ready to Ring II	Martha L. Thompson/Frances L. Callahan	2	Agape	1168
Ready to Ring III	Martha L. Thompson/Frances L. Callahan	3/5	Agape	1198
Clapper Classics	Martha L. Thompson/Frances L. Callahan	2	Agape	1253
Clapper Classics	Martha L. Thompson/Frances L. Callahan	3	Agape	1254
More Clapper Classics	Martha L. Thompson/Frances L. Callahan	3	Agape	1276
Classic Rings	Martha L. Thompson/Frances L. Callahan	3	Agape	1662
Key Rings	Martha L. Thompson/Frances L. Callahan	3 w/keybd		1347/1348
More Key Rings	Martha L. Thompson/Frances L. Callahan	3 w/keybd		1579/1601
Practical Exercises for Developing Rapid Ringing	Martha L. Thompson/Frances L. Callahan		Jeffers	JH S9009E
Developing Coordination Skills	Michael R. Keller		AGEHR	AG001
Developing More Advanced Coordination Skills	Michael R. Keller		AGEHR	AG002
Handbell Assignment Book	Robert Ivey		Agape	1632
Handbell Ringing	Robert Ivey		Hope	1838
Rehearsal Planning, Techniques & Procedure	Michael R. Keller		AGEHR	JHR201
Scoring for English Handbells	Douglas E. Wagner		Agape	1209
Six-In-Hand Techniques	Fred Merrett		Jeffers	JH S9148
Learning to Ring	Janet Van Valey/Susan Berry		Lorenz	
Ringing for the First Time	D. Linda McKechnie		Harold Flammer	HL-5232
Ringing for the First Time -Directors Supplement	D. Linda McKechnie		Harold Flammer	HL-5233
Classics In Bronze	arr. Douglas E. Wagner	3	Lorenz	20/10422
Busy Ringers Series – Collection 1	Kirtsy Mitchell		AGEHR	AG003
Busy Ringers Series – Collection 2	Kirtsy Mitchell		AGEHR	AG004
Busy Ringers Series – Collection 3	Kirtsy Mitchell		AGEHR	AG005
Busy Ringers Series – Collection 4	Kirtsy Mitchell		AGEHR	AG006
Busy Ringers Series – Challenges	Kirtsy Mitchell		AGEHR	AG007
Mastering Musicianship in Handbells	Don Allured		Broadman	
HandChimes in General Music (Grades 1-3) & (Grades 4-6)	Van Valey/Avery		AGEHR	

Appendix C
Suggested Listening List

TITLE	PERFORMING GROUP
Agape Ringers in Concert, The	Agape Ringers
Ain't Misbehavin'	Classical Bells of Detroit
Bell Noel	Campanile Ringers
Bronzeworks	Desert Bells International
Carol On	Strikepoint
Christmas with All the Bells and Whistles	The Jubilation Ringers
Christmas with Sonos	Sonos Handbell Ensemble
Classical Sounds	Sonos Handbell Ensemble
Copper Tin Alloy	Campanile Ringers
Dallas Handbell Ensemble, The	The Dallas Handbell Ensemble
Grand Bells & Brass of Christmas	The Jubilation Ringers
Impressions of the Seasons	The Raleigh Ringers
Point of No Return	Campanile Ringers
Raleigh Ringers, The	The Raleigh Ringers
Ringing Wet/Live at the Coppertop	Strikepoint
Ringside	Strikepoint
Sonos Handbell Ensemble	Sonos Handbell Ensemble
Textures	The Dallas Handbell Ensemble
Toll Away Zone	Twin Cities Handbell Ensemble

Appendix D

Assessment Tools

Dear Parents,

It is appropriate that parents be informed of their child's progress in Honor Bell Ringers. The standards are comprehensive: the outcome or end result is characteristic of a student who demonstrates a high level of skill in playing handbells, poise and confidence and self-discipline in performance, rehearsal and other situations.

The expectations are listed below with the observed behavior which supports learning marked accordingly. It is our hope that this communication be received in the same spirit in which it is offered, with concern for the growth and well-being of the student. The ratings are given with encouragement to continue striving toward the high standards of Honor Bell Ringers.

Key: 4 Exceeds standard
      3 Meets standard, well done
      2 Some progression: needs to keep working
      1 Area of concern

	1st Quarter			2nd Quarter			3rd Quarter			4th Quarter		
	1	2	3	1	2	3	1	2	3	1	2	3
A.												
B.												
C.												
D.												
E.												
F.												
G.												
H.												
I.												
J.												
K.												
L.												

A. Shows responsibility in attendance/promptness to rehearsals and performances

B. Shows initiative and dependability with assigned jobs

C. Demonstrates care of equipment, uniform, music, etc.

D. Displays an understanding of music notation and the ability to apply it

E. Shows improvement in handbell chime ringing skill(s)

F. Has a positive attitude/is enthusiastic

G. Demonstrates appreciation of the Arts

H. Respects the rights, diversity, and feelings of others

I. Accepts responsibility for own learning, shows self-discipline in practicing

J. Listens quietly to and follows directions

K. Handles conflicts appropriately

L. Shows creativity

Comments:_____

_____

_____

You are encouraged to observe rehearsals and discuss with your child his/her progress. Thank you for your support.

HONOR BELL RINGERS AUDITION CRITERIA

Rating: 1 Concern/lacking skill
       2 Possible selection: intensive
          teaching/experience needed
       3 Some potential
       4 Strong audition

Student's Name_____
Grade_____
Homeroom _____
Parent's Name_____
Home Phone #_____
Audition permission form: YES   NO

BELL RINGING PERFORMANCE	1	2	3	4
A. Student can hold bell(s) independently in both hands				
B. Student can control volume of handbells with varied degrees of strength and vigor				
C. Student demonstrates skill in using various handbell-playing techniques:				
ring				
damp				
thumb damp				
shake				
pluck				
martellato				
martellato lift				
malleting				
four in hand				
shelly				
D. Student demonstrates competency in switching bells				
E. Student demonstrates problem solving ability with set up of bells for a difficult passage				
RHYTHMIC COMPETENCY				
F. Student demonstrates ability to maintain a steady beat				
G. Student demonstrates knowledge of music notation:				
note and rest values				
time signatures				
tempo markings and changes				
H. Student demonstrates eye and hand coordination:				
right and left				
able to play different rhythms in each hand simultaneously				
MUSIC READING				
I. Student can track from L to R and possesses the ability to read ahead				
J. Student demonstrates knowledge of 𝄞 and 𝄢 and note letter names on the staff				
K. Student demonstrates knowledge of key signatures, dynamic markings, and music symbols				
L. Student can define/demonstrate handbell symbols: ▼, +, LV, ⊕, TD, •, BD, RT, SK				

	1	2	3	4
M. Student demonstrates sight-reading ability:				
note accuracy				
rhythm accuracy				
tone control				
flow				
damping				
ability to follow the director				
BEHAVIORS SUPPORTING LEARNING				
N. Works independently				
O. Works cooperatively				
P. Respects adults				
Q. Takes care of school/music property				
R. Listens to and follows directions				
S. Adapts easily to situations/others				

INTERVIEW

T. Music background: _____

U. Handbell experience: _____

V. Used what bell distribution system: _____

W. Student commitment/enthusiasm: _____

X. Parent commitment and support:_____

COMMENTS: _____

_____

_____

_____

_____

_____

_____

Appendix E

Handbell Music Publishers

It is not possible to give a suggested repertoire list that would be current and representative of the many fine musicians composing music for handbells. Following is a list of publishers of handbell music. Contact the individual publishers to obtain catalogues and music sample tapes. AGEHR provides a list of handbell composers that are active in their Composers Forum. For a listing of those composers, contact the AGEHR office in Dayton, Ohio, at 937-438-0085.

AGEHR Publishing
911 Neil Avenue, Columbus, Ohio 43215-1334   614-294-2733

Alfred Publishing Company
921 North Grand Avenue, Sherman, Texas 75090   903-868-2143

Art Masters Studios, Inc.
1599 SE 8th Street, Minneapolis, Minnesota 55414   612-378-0027

Augsburg Fortress Publishing Company
P.O. Box 1209, Minneapolis, Minnesota 55440   800-328-4648

Beckenhorst Press, Inc.
P.O. Box 14273, Columbus, Ohio 43214   614-451-6461

Bell Canto Press   800-482-3772
P.O. Box 9189, Spokane, Washington 99209   509-327-3772

Bronze FX
14384 Anchor Lane, Grass Valley, California 95945   530-272-6228

Bronze Handbell Publishers
535 Centre Street, Ashland, Pennsylvania 17921   717-875-1516

Cantabile Press
23 Vista Del Golfo, Long Beach, California 90803   310-433-0334

Choristers Guild
2834 West Kingsley Road, Garland, Texas 75041   214-271-1521

Composers Music Co.
212 Metcalf Street, New Bern, North Carolina 28562   919-638-5295

Concordia Publishing House
3558 South Jefferson Avenue, St. Louis, Missouri 63118   800-325-3040

Doxology Music
P.O. Box M, Aiken, South Carolina 29802   803-649-1733

Flagstaff Publishing
    3875 Apache Court, Boulder, Colorado 80303   303-489-4001

Genovox Music Group
    127 Ninth Avenue, Nashville, Tennessee 37234   615-251-3770

G.I.A. Publications, Inc.
    7404 South Mason, Chicago, Illinois 60638   800-442-1358

Green Rose Press, Inc.
    3116 North Federal Highway, Lighthouse Point, Florida 33064   305-480-2778

Harold Flammer/Shawnee Press, Inc.
    Delaware Water Gap, Pennsylvania 18327   800-962-8584

Hope Publishing Company
    380 South Main Place, Carol Stream, Illinois 60188   800-323-1049

Jeffers Handbell Supply
    P.O. Box 1728, Irmo, South Carolina 29063   800-547-2355

Lake State Publications
    P.O. Box 1593, Grand Rapids, Michigan 49501   616-791-0066

Laurendale Associates
    15035 Wyandotte Street, Van Nuys, California 91405   818-994-6920

Lorenz Corporation
    P.O. Box 802, Dayton, Ohio 45401-0802   800-444-1144

Meredith Music Publishers
    c/o Gold Coast Music Co., 2901 Central Avenue, Alameda, California 94501   888-522-4652

Morning Star Publishers
    1727 Larkin Williams Road, Fenton, Missouri 63026   800-647-2117

National Music Publishers
    16605 Townhouse Drive, Tustin, California 92680   714-542-6266

Psaltery Music Publications
    P.O. Box 181778, Dallas, Texas 75228   214-328-9555

Red River Music
    316 Dublin, Tyler, Texas 75703   903-839-8779

Robert Groth Publications
    46 Hemlock Drive, Deep River, Connecticut 06417   203-526-2802

Soundforth Music
    Bob Jones University, Greenville, South Carolina 29614   800-845-5731

Stained Glass Music
    178 West 11th Street, Holland, Michigan 49423   616-392-6855

Theodore Presser Co.
    Presser Place, Bryn Mawr, Pennsylvania 19010   215-525-3636

Appendix F

Notation Symbols Used In Book

A Glossary of Terms for Handbell and Handchime Ringing Used In This Book

Modern Terminology

Brush Damp	**BD**
Damp Sign	⊕
Echo	↻
Gyro	↻
Handbells	**HB**
Handchimes	**HC**
Hand Damp	**HD**
Notehead shape used for a Handchimes part to distinguish it from a Handbell part when both are notated on the same staff.	♩ ♩
Let Vibrate or *Laissez Vibrer*	**LV**
Mallet on suspended handbell	+
Mallet with handbell on table	⁺•
Mallet Lift	⁺•↑
Mallet Roll on suspended handbell	⁐°⁺

Mallet Roll with handbell on table

Martellato   ▼

Martellato Lift   ▼↑

Pluck   **PL**

Pluck Lift   **PL •↑**

Ring   **R**

Ring Touch   **RT**

Shake   **SK or** ~~~~~~

Swing   **SW or ↑↓**

Thumb Damp   **TD**

Table Land Damp   **TLD**

Tap Pluck   **TPL**

Vibrato   *vib.*

Archaic Terminology

Bells Used Chart. Now referred to as HUC (Handbells Used Chart).   **BUC**

Echo   ↕

Let Vibrate Until Harmony Changes   **LVUHC**

Swing   **Toll**

Tower Swing or Swing   **TS**

Appendix G

For Further Reading

Allured, Donald E. *Mastering Musicianship in Handbells*. Broadman Press, 4591-54, Nashville, Tennessee, 1992.

Behnke, John A. *Successful Ringing: Step By Step*. Concordia Publishing House, 99-1678, St. Louis, Missouri, 1999.

Chanpagne, Aaron. *We Can All Ring: Using Kodaly Hand Signals with Special Handbell Choirs*. The American Guild of English Handbell Ringers, Inc., Dayton, Ohio, 1993.

Ivey, Robert. *Handbell Assignment Book*. Agape-Hope Publishing Company, 1632, Carol Stream, Illinois, 1993.

Keller, Michael R. *Developing Conducting Skills for Directors of Handbell Choirs*. American Guild of English Handbell Ringers, Inc., Dayton, Ohio, 1992.

Keller, Michael R. *Rehearsal Planning, Techniques and Procedures for Directors of Handbell Choirs*. American Guild of English Handbell Ringers, Inc., Dayton, Ohio, 1992.

Keller, Michael R. *Score Study Techniques and Their Application to Rehearsing Handbell Choirs*. American Guild of English Handbell Ringers, Inc., Dayton, Ohio, 1992.

Lorenz, Ellen Jane. *A Manual of Handbell Ringing*. Lorenz Publishing Company, Dayton, Ohio, 1980.

MacGorman, Venita. *The Director As Teacher: Working with the Beginning Handbell Choir*. American Guild of English Handbell Ringers, Inc., Dayton, Ohio, 1993.

McGrew, Letha. *Adaptive Notation for Handbells*. American Guild of English Handbell Ringers, Inc., Dayton, Ohio, 1993.

McKechnie, D. Linda. *Ringing for the First Time*. Harold Flammer, Inc., Shawnee Press, Inc., HL 5232/5233, Delaware Water Gap, Pennsylvania, 1987.

Salzwedel, James V. *A Basic Approach to Handbell Ringing*. Hussite Bell Ringers, Inc., Winston-Salem, North Carolina, 1979.

Thompson, Martha Lynn. *Bell, Book and Ringer*. Harold Flammer, Inc., Shawnee Press, Inc., Delaware Water Gap, Pennsylvania, 1982.

Van Valey, Janet. *Learning to Ring Series*. Lorenz Publishing Company, Dayton, Ohio, 1988.

Appendix H
List of Figures, References

Figure 2.1   traditional, "Teddy Bear"

Figure 2.2   spiritual, "All Night, All Day"

Figure 2.3   McKechnie, D. Linda, *Sarasponda, Ringing for the First Time*, Harold Flammer, HL5232, 3 Oct.

Figure 2.4   McKechnie, D. Linda, *Sarasponda, Ringing for the First Time*, Harold Flammer, HL5232, 3 Oct.

Figure 2.5   Wilson, John F., *Kum Ba Ya*, Agape, #1650, 2-3 Oct.

Figure 2.6   Joplin, Scott, arr. Sharon Elery Rogers, *The Entertainer*, Jeffers, JH S9183, 4-5 Oct.

Figure 2.7   Morris, Hart, *Antiphonal Alleluia*, AGEHR, 570061.

Figure 2.8   traditional, "Alleluia (Canon)"

Figure 2.9   Thompson, Martha Lynn, *Damp Your Bells, Time to Ring*, Agape, 1873

Figure 2.10   Haydn, Franz Joseph, arr. Kevin McChesney, *Surprise Symphony*, Belwin Mills, WBHB9607, 3-5 Oct.

Figure 2.11   Rachmaninoff, Serge, trans. Hart Morris, *Rhapsody on a Theme of Paganini*, Harold Flammer, HP 5177, 3-5 Oct.

Figure 2.12   Kinyon, Barbara Baltzer, *Fiesta*, Harold Flammer, HP 5344, 3-6 Oct.

Figure 2.13   Buckwalter, Karen, *Allegro Festivo*, Harold Flammer, HP 5214, 3-5 Oct.

Figure 2.14   traditional, "Star Light, Star Bright"

Figure 2.15   traditional, "Alleluia (Canon)"

Figure 2.16   Thompson, Martha Lynn, *Jacob's Ladder, Ready to Ring III*, Agape, 1198, 3-5 Oct.

Figure 2.17   Bach, J. S., arr. Barbara Kinyon, *Sheep May Safely Graze*, Beckenhorst Press, HB116, 3-4 Oct + Keyboard.

Figure 2.18   Dobrinski, Cynthia, *Seasonal Procession (for Christmas or Easter)*, Agape, 1394, 3 Oct + Choir.

Figure 2.19   Hilty, Everett Jay, *Echo Rondo*, Posthorn Press, B1005, 4 Oct and 3 Oct.

Figure 2.20   Rawlinson, Tammy W., *Bandelier*, Harold Flammer, HP 5169, 3-4 Oct.